TEN YEARS
IN NORTHERN
IRELAND

The legal control
of political violence

Kevin Boyle
University College, Galway

Tom Hadden
The Queen's University of Belfast

Paddy Hillyard
University of Bristol

The Cobden Trust
1980

Printed in Great Britain by the Russell Press, Nottingham.

CONTENTS

We are grateful to the staff at the Crumlin Road Courthouse in Belfast for their continuing co-operation, to students at Queen's University, Belfast and the University of Bristol for their assistance in the collection and processing of our data, to the Cobden Trust for assistance with the expenses of our work, and to all those who have made comments and criticisms of earlier drafts of this book. As many of those who have helped most have asked not to be identified and as others would not agree with everything we say, it would be invidious to mention any names. We are particularly grateful to Janet McMaw for her remarkable patience and efficiency in dealing with a constant stream of amendments and with the problems of communication between Belfast, Bristol and Galway.

October 1980   *Tom Hadden*
                                                                      Paddy Hillyard
                                                                      Kevin Boyle

The Cobden Trust would like to express its warm thanks to the International League for Human Rights and especially its former chairman, Jerome Shestack, for their financial support and encouragement for this work.

1. INTRODUCTION

It is over ten years since the current emergency in Northern Ireland began. It is five years since the last major review of the impact of emergency security powers was completed. In January 1975 the Gardiner Committee concluded that internment without trial should not be indefinitely prolonged. Internment was accordingly gradually phased out in the course of 1975. Though the power to intern without trial has been retained, it has not been used since. Instead the security forces have relied exclusively on the 'ordinary' criminal process. Some people hoped that the replacement of a 'military security' strategy by a 'police prosecution' strategy would lead to the gradual elimination of terrorist activity. That hope has not been realised. The determination and capacity of the IRA to continue its campaign has been amply demonstrated. Few people now look forward with confidence to any immediate end to the emergency.

This book is a continuation of our earlier studies, *Justice in Northern Ireland: a study in social confidence*[1] and *Law and State: the case of Northern Ireland.*[2] Like them it is based on a detailed empirical investigation of the outcome of a sample of cases dealt with in the courts. In presenting our findings, however, we have been equally concerned to give a more general picture of how the new security strategy has been implemented over the past few years and to distinguish the rhetoric of the politicians and judges from the reality of army and police activity.

Our principal focus in this study has been on the traditional civil libertarian concerns about individual justice and communal discrimination. But we have also been concerned with some issues of broader significance. In the first place we have attempted to explain why the emergency has lasted so long. This can be answered in part only by a consideration of socio-economic and political factors which fall outside the main focus of our study. But we are satisfied that certain aspects of the security operation have made a significant contribution to the lengthy duration of the conflict. In the second place we have attempted to show how certain emergency powers and practices have come to be

5

regarded as almost normal, and to stress how closely the development of these powers and practices is paralleled in other jurisdictions where there is no equivalent pressure of continuing political violence. In this respect our findings are as significant to other common law jurisdictions as they are to Northern Ireland. Our conclusions on the extent to which the criminal process has been 'bureaucratised' and the extent to which effective decision making on guilt or innocence has been shifted back from the court-room to the police-station are of particular relevance to the current debate in Britain on the proceedings of the Royal Commission on Criminal Procedure.

These concerns may seem unduly narrow to those of our readers who would have preferred an analysis which offered some solution to the Northern Ireland problem or some general theoretical explanation of the conflict here, or even of the general role of state power in dealing with political violence. The view that there can only be a political solution to the Northern Ireland conflict – which can usually be interpreted as meaning a political solution which moves towards the reunification of Northern Ireland and the Republic of Ireland – is widespread. So too is criticism by the left of civil libertarian concerns. The following quotation is fairly typical:

> The weakness of the civil libertarian strategy is the assumption that the form of bourgeois legality in Northern Ireland can be similar to that in Britain. Undoubtedly there is some mileage in arguing that because Northern Ireland is part of the United Kingdom universality of Law should apply. But recent history has demonstrated the limitations of the argument. Fundamentally these lie in the class and sectarian nature of the Northern Ireland statelet.[3]

In academic circles there has been a similar resurgence of interest in theoretical explanations of the nature of state power as opposed to more limited empirical accounts of its use in particular circumstances.

We share the general political and academic concern with all these issues. But we make no apology for focusing our account on traditional civil libertarian issues. The rights of individual citizens and of groups or communities are worthy of very careful consideration in their own right. This is especially the case where as in Ireland a substantial communal minority must for the foreseeable future find itself in a state which it would prefer not to be in. This applies equally to the existing Catholic minority in Northern Ireland and to the potential Protestant minority in a reunited Ireland. We do not accept the view that the commitment of the Roman Catholic minority to achieving its aspirations and the readiness of some of its members to resort to political violence is inherently greater than the commitment of the Protestant majority to maintaining the status quo or than the readiness of some members of that community to resort to political violence. Nor do we accept the

6

view that it is impossible to resolve some of the problems which have given rise to the conflict in Northern Ireland within a Northern Ireland or a British state. The political and social changes which would be necessary to achieve a stable and peaceful state within Northern Ireland are not in our view of a different order from those which would be necessary to achieve a stable and peaceful all-Ireland state.

On the broader issue of state power, we hope to show through our account of what has been happening in Northern Ireland how difficult it is to talk in terms of simple state power, as if the state were independent of the various bureaucratic organs which act for it. Our object is to explain some of the mechanisms through which abuses of state power may be engendered. Our analysis in this respect transcends the problems which face the state in Northern Ireland.

For all these reasons we stand by our limited and detailed analysis and critique of the application of both 'emergency' and 'ordinary' powers by the organs of the state. Analysis and critique of this kind is essential both in terms of making workable proposals for constructive changes in law and practice and of understanding the reality of the criminal process, and through it of state power, in Northern Ireland and elsewhere.

2. THE BACKGROUND
Socio-economic Factors
in the Northern Ireland Conflict

In our previous studies we have given a detailed account of the genesis of the current round in the Northern Ireland conflict. In this chapter our objective is to give some indication of the socio-economic factors which have contributed to the prolongation of that conflict. In any general account of the situation in Northern Ireland, however, it is essential to stress some basic facts.

In the first place there is in Northern Ireland as presently constituted an overwhelming majority in favour of maintaining the constitutional union with Britain. In communal terms there are almost one million Protestants who generally support the link with Britain and just over half a million Roman Catholics who generally favour the reunification of Ireland. In the last direct and formal vote on the matter in March 1973 58 per cent of the electorate voted to support the union with Britain; less than one per cent voted for a united Ireland; and 41 per cent did not vote.[1] Though there are a few Protestant Republicans and perhaps rather more Catholics who are prepared to support the union with Britain, it is undeniable that attitudes and voting on this basic issue of national allegiance must be accounted for in communal rather than class terms. In both communities the prevailing political allegiance includes both middle and working classes, and is strengthened by effective educational segregation in primary and secondary schools.

There are nonetheless important socio-economic differences between the two communities. Though each supports a prosperous professional middle class, certain types of economic activity and employment, notably banking, commerce and engineering, are predominantly Protestant, while certain others, notably construction and the service industries, are predominantly Catholic. There has in addition been a consistently higher rate of unemployment among Catholics than among Protestants. This was in part due to deliberate discrimination under the Unionist regime.[2] But it was also due in part to underlying structural factors linked to patterns of education and expectations of discrimination. Whatever the explanation, it is clear that growing dissatisfaction with their position and the demand for greater equality in employment, housing and other spheres was the primary cause of the development of the civil rights movement among Catholics in Northern Ireland.

The civil rights campaign was directed primarily against alleged discrimination by Unionists in central and local government. It met with little initial success and, as confrontations with opposing groups of extreme Protestants and with the police became more and more frequent, peaceful marches and demonstrations developed into communal rioting and eventually into guerrilla warfare. The failure of the Unionist government to deal effectively with the deteriorating situation, despite the commitment of British troops in August 1969, eventually led to the suspension of the Stormont regime in March 1972. Since then there have been eight years of 'direct rule' from Westminster broken only by a few months of devolved government on non-security matters by the short-lived power-sharing Executive in 1974.

The most pressing concern of the British administration during most of this period has been with security. But it has also been committed to eliminating any remaining discriminatory practices and to the unbiased allocation of public resources. An impressive range of governmental and autonomous agencies has been established with the specific purpose of remedying and preventing discrimination in public administration at all levels and in employment.[3] Much time and energy has been devoted to securing proper and effective representation of the minority community on official bodies. And the level of public spending in Northern Ireland has, in the past, grown much more rapidly than in other parts of the United Kingdom.[4]

It is hard to deny the good intentions of the Westminster government in this sphere. It is equally hard to identify any significant improvement in the relative position of Catholics in socio-economic terms. Levels of unemployment, poverty and general deprivation in Catholic areas in Belfast and in the west of the Province are significantly higher than in Protestant areas.

The differences in unemployment rates are easy to establish.[5] The overall unemployment rate for Northern Ireland during the period of our survey in 1979 varied between 10% and 12%. In the largely Catholic employment districts of Londonderry, Strabane and Newry the figures were 15%, 24% and 20%; in the predominantly Protestant districts of Ballymena, Craigavon and Coleraine they were 11%, 9% and 12%. In Belfast itself the overall unemployment rate was 9%. But the position within the city mirrors that elsewhere in the Province, as shown in the *Belfast Housing Survey* carried out by the Northern Ireland Housing Executive in 1978.[6] The survey revealed an overall unemployment rate for heads of household — a slightly different measure from that given above — of 14% for the whole of Belfast. In the almost exclusively Catholic wards in West and North Belfast the corresponding figures were very much greater: in Whiterock it was 49%, in New Lodge 41%, in Falls 51% and in Clonard 35%. In all there were eleven Catholic wards in which the figure was more than 20%. There were only four such wards in predominantly Protestant or mixed wards: the highest figure was for Crumlin at 27%, followed by Highfield with 25%, Ballymacarret with 21% and North Howard with 20%.

There are a number of underlying reasons for these differences. In the first place the Unionist government before 1969 consistently pursued economic policies, particularly in the siting of new industrial developments, which benefited Protestant areas. In the second place a major part of the labour market was controlled by Protestants. As a result employment opportunities for Protestants have long been better than those for Catholics. The Westminster government has attempted to restore the balance since 1972. But it has proved inherently more difficult to create new jobs in specifically Catholic areas, particularly in the most troubled areas like West Belfast, than in relatively prosperous employment centres like Craigavon and Ballymena/Antrim.

The troubles themselves have clearly aggravated the problem. Many Catholics were driven out of mixed areas in 1972 and 1973 and took refuge in West Belfast and other 'safe' Catholic enclaves.[7] They remain reluctant to travel to work in areas which they regard as predominantly Protestant or to apply for or accept jobs in firms in which there is a tradition of militant loyalism. The Fair Employment Agency has on a number of occasions induced employers with a largely or exclusively Protestant workforce to take on a few Catholics, only to find that they have almost immediately given up their new jobs in the face of real or imagined intimidation.

There have also been significant changes in the class structure of the two communities. Over the last 70 years the proportion of Catholics in semi-skilled manual and non-manual occupations has declined and the proportion in unskilled and manual occupations has increased.[8] At the other end of the scale the proportion of Catholics in professional and managerial occupations has increased. Though the statistical evidence is inconclusive on this point, the expansion of the Catholic middle class appears to have been particularly rapid in the 1960s and 1970s as opportunities for employment in the professions and the public sector increased. These trends are in sharp contrast with those in the Protestant community, in which there has been a decline in both unskilled and skilled manual occupations and a corresponding increase in other categories. Though the precise impact of these changes is hard to assess, it seems likely that the increase in the proportion of Catholics in unskilled occupations and the decline in the proportion of Protestants in that category has been an important factor in the continuing conflict.

The differential in unemployment rates clearly contributes to the high level of financial deprivation in many Catholic areas. A large proportion of families in such areas are wholly or partly dependent on social security payments.[9] This means that a relatively high proportion of Catholics are living on incomes which are on or below the official subsistence rate for the United Kingdom. The situation is aggravated by two factors which are peculiar to Northern Ireland. In the first place the structure of social security benefits is settled within the UK as a whole. But rents in Northern Ireland are generally lower than in Britain and charges for electricity and gas are appreciably higher. This means that households living on supplementary benefit in Northern Ireland are relatively worse off than their counterparts in Britain, since assistance towards rent is fixed at the actual amount of rent payable while assistance towards heating and lighting is included in the overall scale rates. In the second place there is a tendency for Catholic families to be somewhat larger than the average for Protestants in Northern Ireland and for the UK as a whole. Figures in the *Belfast Household Survey* for 1978 showed that 13 Catholic wards had above average proportions for households with four or more children compared with only four other wards, and that in these wards about one in ten families had four or more children compared with an average figure of one in 20 for the whole of Belfast.[10] There was a similar concentration of very large families with six or more children in Catholic wards. This too contributes to the general level of deprivation since it is generally recognised that families with large numbers of children find it difficult to make ends meet because of the inadequacy of scale rates. It is also difficult for heads of such households to earn as much as they would receive from social security, given the relatively low level of wages in Northern Ireland as a whole.[11]

As a result of this combination of factors many families in Catholic areas are caught up in accumulated debts for rent, electricity and gas, and are thus subject to the penal effects of the emergency debt collection system introduced under the Payment for Debt (Emergency Provisions) Act (N.I.) 1971 to counter the rent and rates strike against internment. This involves the compulsory deduction at source of a proportion of social security payments to meet both accrued and current debts to statutory bodies. This system has been continued despite the fact that the strike in respect of which it was introduced was called off as long ago as 1974, and was extended in 1976 to cover gas and electricity debts. Some measure of relief from the most penal aspects of the system was introduced early in 1980 in response to widespread concern among social workers and others at the effects of expecting the most deprived families to live on less than minimum subsistence incomes. But the continued application of the system has undoubtedly increased the sense of alienation from the organs of government among those affected by it.

A final factor is the depressing environment and quality of life in many Catholic estates and districts. Official figures on the physical condition of housing reveal very high levels of unfitness in inner city areas in both Catholic and Protestant districts. For instance, in 1978 seven Protestant wards compared with five Catholic wards had fewer than 60% of houses with all five basic amenities.[12] But the scale of environmental deterioration in the Catholic areas is observably greater. This is largely a result of the continuing IRA campaign and the resulting confrontations between local youths and the security forces. The bulk of IRA bombs are directed against property which is close to or even within the major Catholic areas. This is probably due to the reluctance of the bombers to stray too far from familiar territory. But whatever the reason it means that the level of destruction in the main centres of Catholic population in West Belfast, Derry, Strabane and Newry is far in excess of that in East Belfast, Ballymena, Bangor and Portadown, the main centres of Protestant population. The main impact of British Army activity, both regular patrols and arrest and follow-up operations, and the 'aggro' which it sometimes sparks off is likewise concentrated in Catholic areas. It is the Catholic rather than the Protestant community which has the most direct and continuing experience of the physical effects of 'the troubles'.

All these factors combine to produce a strong feeling of continuing deprivation and discrimination among many Catholics, particularly those in the most troubled areas. The Westminster government has made strenuous efforts to remedy the situation. It is now the policy of the Department of Commerce to concentrate expenditure on the creation of new jobs on the areas of highest unemployment in west Belfast and the west of the Province. Incoming firms are offered substantial inducements to site their factories in these areas. There have also been repeated campaigns to improve the physical environment both in the Province as a whole and in the worst affected areas. But the social and economic forces which we have outlined have for the most part proved stronger than the capacity of the government, however well-meaning, to counteract them.

The reality remains that, in comparison with Protestants, working class Catholics in Northern Ireland are no better off under direct rule from Westminster than they were under the Unionist regime. Many are worse off in both relative and absolute terms. This naturally reinforces their underlying alienation from the state in Northern Ireland and helps to maintain their commitment to the ideals of Republicanism and Irish unity. It accordingly increases the difficulties faced by the British government in seeking to promote a political settlement within the framework of the existing constitutional position. For the reasons we have explained we do not intend to embark on an outline of political developments since the creation and fall of the so-called 'power-sharing' Executive in 1974. It is sufficient for our purposes to emphasise that the continuing deprivation and discrimination experienced by Catholics

and the continuing political stalemate provides an ideal environment for
continuing recruitment by the IRA.

3. THE PARAMILITARIES
Republican and Loyalist Groups

There has been a remarkable stability in the nature of the conflict in Northern Ireland in the past five or six years. In the initial period of the civil rights movement and the ensuing 'troubles' the main focus of attention, as described in *Law and State,* was on the continuing confrontations on the streets, both between rival groups of Catholics and Protestants and between Catholics — and occasionally Protestants — and the security forces. In this early period there were relatively few bombings and shootings. The decision to introduce internment without trial in August 1971 sparked off a massive increase in organised guerrilla activity on what is now best called the Republican side. This was directed primarily against the security forces and public or semi-public buildings like large shops and hotels. The suspension of Stormont and the imposition of direct rule from Westminster early in 1972 sparked off a corresponding increase in activity on what is now best called the Loyalist side. This was directed primarily against Catholics, both in terms of intimidation of individual families living in mixed areas and of bombing and shooting attacks on Catholic public houses and on individual Catholics.[1] Though there have been frequent variations in the intensity of activity on either side, both in response to political developments and as a result of negotiated or unilateral cease-fires, there has been a progressive decline in the level of these activities from a peak in 1972, as shown in Table 3.1. But the essential nature of terrorist activity on either side has not altered.

The purpose of this chapter is to attempt to explain this relative stability in terms of the organisation and recruitment of activists on either side. We can claim no special inside knowledge of terrorist organisations or activities. But a good deal of useful and generally reliable information has emerged from our study of cases which have come before the courts. If this is combined with the detailed factual information on the background of convicted offenders and with generally accepted descriptions of the way in which the IRA and their Loyalist counterparts operate, a reasonably accurate picture can be constructed.

Though it was Loyalists who first resorted to violence in the present

14

Table 3.1: Official figures on the incidence of terrorist activity
in Northern Ireland from 1969 to 1979

	1969	1970	1971	1972	1973	1974
Shootings	na	213	1756	10628	5018	3206
Explosions	8	155	1033	1495	1007	669
Soldiers killed	–	–	43	103	58	28
RUC/UDR killed	1	2	16	43	21	22
Civilians killed	12	23	115	321	171	166

	1975	1976	1977	1978	1979
Shootings	1803	1908	1081	755	728
Explosions	366	663	366	455	422
Soldiers killed	14	14	15	14	38
RUC/UDR killed	17	38	28	17	24
Civilians killed	216	245	69	50	51

*Source: Royal Ulster Constabulary: these figures differ slightly from those
published by the Army.*

round of troubles, both in terms of attacks on civil rights demonstrators
and in terms of the first bombings in 1969, it is more realistic to deal
first with Republican organisations.[2] The IRA in its various forms has
been the primary motive force in embarking on and sustaining a guerrilla
campaign directed against the British presence in Ireland and against the
continued existence of a separate state in Northern Ireland. Loyalist
organisations, notably the UVF and the UDA, are best regarded as a
response to the perceived threat from the IRA.

The IRA

To understand the present structure of the IRA it is essential to outline
briefly the recent history of the Republican movement.[3] The IRA are
the successors of the militant faction within the guerrilla army which
fought the British in the Irish war of independence in 1919 and 1920.
That conflict was resolved by a political settlement in 1920 which
included the partition of Ireland and the dismantling of the republic
declared in Dublin in 1919. The resistance by the IRA to the terms of
the 1920 settlement led directly to the outbreak of civil war in the
south of Ireland in 1922 and 1923, and later to sporadic campaigns by
the IRA, notably in 1938 and 1956-62, designed to end partition and
to complete the process of British withdrawal from Ireland.

In the 1960s the leaders of the Republican movement abandoned
the strategy of pursuing their objectives by military force and joined in
the general campaign for civil rights and social justice within Northern
Ireland. When this campaign eventually led to serious sectarian violence
in the summer of 1969, however, there was substantial pressure both
from Catholics in Northern Ireland and from their supporters in the

Republic to rebuild an effective fighting force, primarily with a view to defending the Catholic community in Northern Ireland. Those individuals in the Republican movement who had opposed the shift from a military to a political strategy seized the opportunity to recommence a military campaign in Northern Ireland. When this policy was repudiated at the Sinn Fein conference in 1970, the militants broke away from the 'official' movement and established a rival 'provisional' movement. These labels — official and provisional — were used by the media to distinguish the two factions and have become established. Since then the Provisional IRA had built up and sustained its campaign both within Northern Ireland and in Britain. The Official IRA maintained its separate existence and mounted its own distinct guerrilla campaign, though on a much less intense level than that of the Provisionals, until 1972. It then declared a unilateral cease-fire on the ground that no further political purpose would be served by continuing in the face of the clear commitment of the majority in Northern Ireland for the status quo. Some members of the Official IRA who were dissatisfied with this decision have since formed themselves into a new force, the Irish National Liberation Army, which is regarded as the military wing of the Irish Republican Socialist Party (IRSP). These three organisations, the Provisionals, the Officials and the IRSP/INLA, have on a number of occasions engaged in open feuding in West Belfast and elsewhere.

These ideological and organisational splits should not be permitted to obscure the essentially communal base of the IRA. Certain families and certain districts have traditionally adhered to one or other wing of the movement. But the underlying strength of the movement as a whole lies in the ability of whichever faction happens to be most active to recruit volunteers for active service.

It is difficult to be precise about how people join the IRA. The picture which emerges from a study of court records is likely to be coloured by what the police believe to be the process of recruitment. This may be termed the 'god-father' view, in which the main emphasis is on active recruitment by existing members of the organisation. In cases of this kind an initial contact is made with boys and girls who are thought likely to be sympathetic to the 'movement'. They are then invited to join the Fianna Eireann, the junior wing of the IRA. But it is likely that the process of recruitment in many cases is closer to what might be termed the 'club' view. In such cases, young boys and girls who are committed to the aims of the movement and attracted by the glamorous nature of its activities seek out a known member of the organisation and ask to join. In the closely integrated communities in working class Catholic areas it is not difficult for those who wish to find an appropriate contact.

When they have been accepted as members, which may involve

swearing a simple oath of loyalty to the movement, new recruits will be asked to carry out such tasks as acting as a scout or reporting on the movement of Army or police patrols in the area. They may also be asked to attend arms training sessions and to march in parades at funerals. It is not clear how far such tasks as selling *Republican News* and joining in weekend 'aggro' and hijackings and burnings on such occasions as the anniversary of internment are part of the specific duties of Fianna members. Youths and girls who could not properly be regarded as members of any organisation certainly take part in such activities on a regular basis. But the ties of membership at this level are relatively loose. It appears to be relatively easy for Fianna members to drift into and out of the movement. There is sometimes strong parental pressure on those who get involved to leave.

Those who progress to membership of the IRA proper, or of its women's branch, the Cumann na mBan, are known as volunteers. There does not appear to be any great formality in graduating from the Fianna to the IRA or the Cumann na mBan. But as reliable and committed recruits grow older they are expected to take part in shooting and bombing operations. They may also be required to carry out punishments by kneecapping or beating both on those members of the movement who have co-operated with the security forces or indulged in 'private' robberies and thefts, and on other youths and adults who are not members of the movement in respect of similar 'offences'. The introduction to activities of this kind is likely to be gradual. In the first instance the volunteer will be asked to play a relatively minor role in the operation, for instance by collecting a gun from a hiding place or disposing of it afterwards. But there is unlikely to be any advance warning when a volunteer is required to take part in the operation itself, as a gunman, driver or lookout. Volunteers are expected to be prepared to kill people and to plant bombs when instructed to do so. It is clear from the pattern of convictions that many of the most serious, and from a non-terrorist point of view horrific operations are carried out by young volunteers without much previous experience. The use of young and readily replaceable volunteers in the majority of operations, as opposed to seasoned and wanted terrorists, is one of the important features of the IRA campaign.

The extent to which women are involved in the IRA is more difficult to determine. In our sample of cases there were only 19 Republican women. Of these about half were charged with serious offences such as planting bombs and incendiaries and the possession of firearms. The rest were charged with relatively minor offences such as scouting, membership and failure to disclose information. This suggests that women play a much smaller role in violent activities than men, and that the pursuit of the IRA's campaign of violence has been a predominantly male activity. The main contribution of women has been supportive rather than active. It seems likely that this is due primarily to the general acceptance of the traditional and passive role of women in Irish society.

It is much more difficult to be precise about the higher levels in the organisation. There has been frequent talk of a change from a standard military formation, with battalions and a clearly defined hierarchy of officers, typical of the IRA in the 1930s and 1950s, to the use of small units or cells in which the members have little or no knowledge of their superiors. It has been said that this change has been one of the most significant factors in counteracting the efforts of the security forces to identify and put behind bars the organisers, or so-called 'godfathers', of the IRA campaign. But the extent of this change has probably been exaggerated. Independent cells have been used for operations in Britain and abroad. In Northern Ireland the organisation of the IRA remains essentially local, with separate operational units in each of the main Republican districts, as for instance in Lower Falls, Turf Lodge/Bally-murphy, Andersonstown, the Markets in Belfast and in Derry, Tyrone and South Armagh. In each district the functions of commanding officer, quartermaster and information officer still appear to be identifiable. The CO issues orders in respect of major province-wide operations, directs the ordinary operations of units in his district, and supervises disciplinary and 'policing' operations. The quartermaster is responsible for the procuring, storing and deploying of arms and explosives. The information officer, who is usually an older man, is responsible for co-ordinating the collection of information on likely targets, and in some areas for recruitment and discipline. None of these officers will usually be directly engaged in offensive operations, with a view to making it difficult for the security forces to gather information of a type which would ensure their conviction in a court of law.

The essentially local base of IRA organisation is confirmed by the pattern of offences covered in our survey. For the most part shootings and bombings, and the less serious offences of hijacking and robbery, are carried out by volunteers in their own home town or district. It is rare for volunteers to be expected to operate far from their own district. The defendants charged for almost all the major terrorist attacks in Belfast covered in our survey lived in Belfast; the pattern in other urban areas was the same. In country areas the pattern was slightly different, but volunteers concentrated their operations on their own market towns. Even in the case of experienced and notorious gunmen, who are 'on the run' or living in the Republic, it is usual for their activities to be restricted to their original home area. This policy or pattern makes some sense. In one of the few cases in our survey in which Belfast volunteers were ordered to carry out a bombing elsewhere, the operation was badly bungled, not least by the fact that the volunteers had to ask the way to their target twice and were thereafter readily identified by witnesses. But it does have the additional effect of ensuring, as already noted, that much of the destruction is concentrated in towns where there is a substantial Catholic population or clientele rather than in predominantly Protestant towns.

Further evidence for this general pattern of recruitment and deployment is provided by the data on the background of Republican offenders covered in our survey (see Table 3.2). More than half (53%) of those who came before the courts were under 21, and a further fifth were aged between 21 and 25; barely one in ten (11%) were over 30. The use of relatively inexperienced volunteers as opposed to hardened 'professional' terrorists is likewise illustrated by the fact that almost half (43%) of those who appeared in the courts had no previous record. Very few had a previous conviction for serious 'ordinary' crime (8%) and only one in ten (11%) had previous convictions for terrorist offences. These results are similar to those of our earlier survey of offenders coming before the courts in 1975.[4] In that period 70% of Republican defendants were under 21, 13% were between 21 and 25, and 55% had no previous record. Given the youth of most of the defendants and the lack of detail on some of the police records on which the study is based it would be unwise to give precise figures on social class and employment record. But we are satisfied that the data establishes beyond reasonable doubt that the bulk of Republican offenders are young men and women without criminal records in the ordinary sense, though some have been involved in public disorders of the kind which frequently take place in the areas in which they live. Both in this respect and in their records of employment and unemployment they are reasonably representative of the working class community of which they form a substantial part. They are recruited as school leavers who feel it to be their duty to assist in continuing the struggle for what they regard as their natural political and socio-economic rights. They do not fit the stereotype of criminality which the authorities have from time to time attempted to attach to them. General communal support for the IRA has undoubtedly declined in recent years. But the pattern of recruitment still demonstrates the essentially communal nature of the movement and its close relationship to the political aspirations of the Catholic community and the continuing deprivation and discrimination which it experiences.

Loyalist groups

The organisation of terrorist activities on the Loyalist side is much less coherent.[5] There are two major organisations which are more or less openly engaged in paramilitary activities, the Ulster Volunteer Force (UVF) and the Ulster Defence Association (UDA). But there are numerous offshoots of these and other groups whose precise status and relationship is often far from clear.

The UVF, like the IRA, can be traced back to the initial stages in the Northern Ireland conflict. Huge numbers of those who opposed the threatened imposition of 'Home Rule' for the whole of Ireland responded to the call by Sir Edward Carson for the formation of a militia to defend the status of Ulster as an integral part of the UK. The Ulster Volunteer Force at that time drew its support from all sections of the Protestant community, both middle and working class. On the formation of the Northern Ireland state, however, much of the work of the original UVF was legitimised. Many of its members joined the newly created 'B Specials', part of the Royal Ulster Constabulary, in 1920.

The UVF thus became little more than a communal memory until it re-emerged as a small underground terrorist group in the 1960s. It was centred on the fiercely Loyalist Shankill Road in Belfast and its membership was essentially working class, with a high proportion of shipyard workers. Its first serious activities were the Malvern Street murders in 1966. Since then the UVF has continued to carry out sporadic attacks on Republican targets and on individual Catholics. It was declared illegal under the Civil Authorities (Special Powers) Act in 1966. Early in 1974 it was deproscribed on the ground that it had moved from terrorist to political activity on the foundation of a political organisation called the Volunteer Party. The leaders of this change in approach, however, were soon deposed and a new terrorist campaign was started by hardliners. The UVF was again declared illegal in 1975.

The Ulster Defence Association is a much larger organisation. It was founded in 1972 as a direct response to the suspension of the Stormont Parliament and rapidly recruited huge numbers of members from the Protestant working classes. Its primary purpose as a mass movement was to demonstrate the scale of opposition in the Protestant community to any movement towards a united Ireland. It openly engaged in drilling and other paramilitary operations and mounted a number of disciplined and impressive demonstrations of its manpower. It also organised large scale vigilante patrolling of the kind which has a long tradition in Ulster. It has never openly engaged in or claimed responsibility for terrorist operations. But within the UDA there were groups which were involved in sectarian killings and other terrorist operations. Members of the UDA also played a significant part in the mass intimidation of Catholics from their homes in mixed areas of Belfast and other towns in 1972 and 1973. And it is an open secret that the Ulster Freedom Fighters (UFF) was little more than a convenient *nom de guerre* for certain UDA members. The UFF and a number of similar organisations, such as the Red Hand Commando have, like the UVF, been formally proscribed. But the UDA itself has never been an unlawful organisation. Since 1977 it has maintained a more or less effective suspension of hostilities, though it has on occasions threatened to resume its operations.

It is more difficult to detect any clearly defined differences in the political approach of these various Loyalist organisations than of their Republican counterparts. As in the case of the various branches of the IRA, there have been periods in which members of the UDA and UVF have engaged in murderous feuds. But this appears to have been more a consequence of disputes over territorial control and racketeering than of differences in political or military strategy. The arguments among Loyalist pressure groups over the relative merits of continued direct rule, devolved government or some form of independence for a new Ulster state have only occasionally been reflected in the public commitments of the UVF or the UDA, as for instance the UVF's brief association with the Volunteer Party in 1974 or the UDA's more recent support for the New Ulster Political Research Group's policies on an independent Ulster. The political position of both groups, however, has not generally been very clear. This is in sharp contrast to both branches of the IRA which have always maintained separate political and military wings and regularly hold annual conferences.

There is somewhat less formal difference in structures on the military side. Both the UVF and the UDA have formal command structures similar to those of the British Army or the IRA. The UDA has a central office and a supreme commander and has been able to mount concerted action in support of a number of province-wide political strikes. But terrorist operations by UDA and UVF members are much less co-ordinated than those of the IRA, which has frequently demonstrated its ability to plan and put into operation concerted campaigns. In practice many offensive operations on the Loyalist side appear to be thought up and planned at relatively short notice by small groups at local drinking clubs. In many instances the operation consists of little more than the theft of a car or motorcycle, driving it into the nearest convenient Catholic area and shooting or bombing a convenient target. In a few cases attacks are more carefully planned and directed against notorious or allegedly notorious IRA members or meeting places. But for the most part those involved appear to consider it to be sufficient for their purposes to shoot at or kill any Catholic whom they happen to come across, as for instance in the case of the notorious Shankill butchers.

The difference in approach to the choice of targets is sometimes used as a justification for claiming that Loyalist terrorist operations are essentially sectarian in contrast to those of the IRA which are claimed to be essentially political. It would be unwise to make too much of this distinction. Much of the difference stems from the nature of the conflict. It is relatively easy for the IRA to select targets which are in some way symbolic of 'British occupation' or of the Unionist regime.

The most obvious are members of the British Army, the UDR and the police. It is also relatively easy to justify more or less random attacks on commercial and industrial property as attacks on 'legitimate economic targets'. It is less easy for Loyalists to select 'legitimate' targets which are not in some way associated with the minority community as such. And for many purposes IRA attacks on members of the UDR and the RUC, particularly those on part-time members while off duty, are no less sectarian in intention or effect. The absence of effective co-ordination and discipline on the Loyalist side, and the reactive nature of their activities are more significant than any alleged ideological differences in the nature of their activities.

The pattern of paramilitary activity on the Loyalist side is also affected by the fact that there are a number of legitimate outlets for those members of the Protestant community who wish to play their part in the fight against the IRA. Many committed Loyalists, who on the Catholic side might be potential members of the IRA, join the RUC Reserve or the UDR. But Loyalists who have criminal records or who are known to be involved in unlawful paramilitary activity are not usually accepted in these forces. There is accordingly a rather higher proportion of members with previous criminal records in the UDA and UVF than might otherwise be expected. This was clearly observable in our 1979 survey of the background of Loyalist offenders. Only a small minority (14%) of defendants on the Loyalist side had no previous police record, compared with 43% of Republican defendants; very many more of the Loyalists (52%) had previous convictions for 'ordinary' crimes than of the Republicans (33%).

Loyalist defendants in 1979 were also likely to be a good deal older than their Republican counterparts. Only a handful (15%) were under 21, compared with more than half (53%) of Republicans; almost half the Loyalists (47%) were more than 25, compared with only a quarter (24%) of Republicans. This age differential is partly due to the absence of any organised recruitment of juveniles on the Loyalist side. It may also be due to changing patterns in the membership of Loyalist groups. Loyalists in our 1975 sample were less likely to have a criminal record: four in ten (39%) were first offenders. And they were generally younger: well over half (56%) were under 21. This difference was probably due to the fact that there was a high level of alienation and paramilitary activity throughout the Protestant community in 1973 and 1974 which was reflected in our 1975 sample of offenders. By 1978, however, there was much less general alienation within the Protestant community. Those who became involved in paramilitary activities then were much less representative of their community. Loyalist youths continued to commit scheduled offences, notably robbery. But they were less likely to be recruited for more serious shooting and bombing operations.

Table 3.2. The age and previous criminal records of Diplock defendants in 1975 and 1979

Age	Loyalists 1975	Loyalists 1979	Republicans 1975	Republicans 1979
14-17	14%	2%	7%	8%
17-21	42%	13%	63%	45%
21-25	11%	28%	13%	19%
25-30	16%	22%	8%	13%
30-40	8%	21%	4%	7%
Over 40	4%	4%	1%	4%
Not known	5%	9%	4%	4%
Record				
None	39%	14%	55%	43%
Non-scheduled*	49%	52%	31%	33%
Scheduled*	5%	13%	7%	11%
Not known	8%	20%	7%	13%

*See p.57 for definition of 'scheduled offence'.

Source: 'Who are the Terrorists?' Fortnight Issue 126, 7 May 1976.

Conclusion

These differences in the recruitment and membership of Republican and Loyalist groups must not be allowed to obscure their essential similarities. Both the IRA and its counterparts are rooted in their respective communities. Both are more permanent than their membership at any given time, in the sense that new leaders and recruits are always coming forward to carry on the traditions that have been established over more than 50 years. Both are concrete expressions of the shared aspirations and concerns of those communities; on the Catholic side aspirations for the unification of Ireland and fears of continued oppression and deprivation, on the Loyalist side fears of absorption in a Catholic dominated Ireland and aspirations for the continued existence of some form — any form — of separate constitutional status for Northern Ireland.

This cultural permanence has important implications for security policy. It means that the elimination of IRA activity and Loyalist reaction to it is not just a matter of arresting and putting behind bars the existing members of the various groups. Terrorist activity can be contained by that means. But it cannot be eliminated as long as the conditions for continued recruitment or regeneration remain. For reasons which we have explained it is not our purpose to discuss the possibilities for a political settlement in Northern Ireland. But as will be seen there are aspects of current security policy which in themselves contribute to the continuation of the conflict.

4. THE SECURITY FORCES
Army and Police Methods

British troops were deployed in Londonderry and Belfast in 1969 to put an end to communal rioting. For reasons which we have attempted to explain in *Law and State* what began as a fairly straightforward peace-keeping operation gradually developed into a series of confrontations between the Army and the civilian population in the main Catholic areas in Belfast and elsewhere, and then into sporadic guerrilla warfare between the IRA and the Army. In 1971 an attempt was made to remedy the situation by a policy of mass internment without trial. In practice the use of internment made matters worse. The initial operation was mishandled, in that large numbers of innocent people were arrested and illtreated. The continuing use of internment by the Army in the case of most Republican suspects while Loyalist suspects were for the most part dealt with by the police and the courts confirmed the feelings in the Catholic community that internment and the military security systems that went with it were discriminatory and unacceptable. Following the recommendation of the Gardiner Committee in 1975 that internment was necessary in the short term but could not be continued as a long term policy, the British government decided to phase it out and to rely exclusively on a policy of prosecuting terrorist suspects in the courts.[1] The last internee was released in December 1975.

This change had important implications for the respective roles of the Army and the police. It has meant the replacement of a security system based upon the identification by military intelligence of active terrorists and their subsequent arrest and detention by a system based upon the collection by the police of sufficient evidence against individuals to merit putting them on trial for specific criminal offences. The essence of the change is neatly illustrated by the change in 1975 in Army statistical terminology from the phrase 'number of terrorists out of action' to that of 'charges for terrorist offences'. It has been associated with a substantial decline in Army numbers and an increasing reliance on local security forces, the so-called policy of Ulsterisation. Total Army numbers have declined from a maximum of 21,000 in 1973 to a current level in 1980 of some 12,000. The combined total of RUC, RUC Reserve and UDR has increased in the same period from 14,500 to 19,500.

The change from military security to police prosecution has nonetheless been a gradual and lengthy process. Many elements of the previous strategy have continued to be applied by the Army. And some have been incorporated into the modified prosecution system operated by the police. The object of this chapter is to describe the changing roles of the Army and the police over the past five years as a preliminary to the more detailed discussion of interrogation and of the working of the Diplock courts in Chapters 5 and 6.

The Army

There have always been British troops in Northern Ireland. Prior to 1969 there was a regular garrison of some 3,000, whose underlying purpose as in other states was to provide a backup for the police in the event of serious public disorder or other emergency, and ultimately to deter or prevent any attempt at a forcible seizure of power from the constitutional authorities.

Table 4.1: Numbers in the security forces in Northern Ireland

	British Army	UDR	B Specials	RUC	RUCR	Total
1969	3000	–	8500	3000	–	14500
1973	16500	7500	–	4500	2500	31000
1980	12000	8000	–	7000	4500	31500

Source: Northern Ireland Information Service.

In 1969 it was the Unionist government which, in accordance with the constitutional proprieties, asked the Westminster government to authorise the use of troops in Londonderry and Belfast. In that initial period the Army simply carried out its role as the state force of last resort for the maintenance of law and order, particularly in those areas where the RUC was unable to operate effectively. The Army's role in the period from 1971, following the decision to introduce internment without trial in August 1971 and the imposition of direct rule from Westminster in March 1972, was entirely different. Its operations were designed primarily to facilitate the collection of intelligence on IRA activity in the main centres of Catholic population and thus to enable IRA activists to be arrested and put behind bars. To this end the Army put into operation a series of techniques which had been used in Malaya, Kenya, Aden and other colonial emergencies and developed by Army theoreticians like Brigadier Frank Kitson.[2] The basis of this system was the creation and maintenance of as complete a dossier as was practicable on all inhabitants of suspect areas so that those who were thought to have become involved in IRA activities could be quickly identified and detained. The principal mechanisms were regular house searches and head counts, frequent arrest and 'screening' of those who might be likely to become involved, and the interrogation in depth of selected suspects.

The system of intelligence gathering was applied on a more or less uniform basis in Catholic districts throughout the Province. Army regiments were expected to maintain regular foot patrols in all suspect areas, not only to prevent the establishment of what became known as 'no-go areas' but also to assist in building up a very detailed picture of the area and its inhabitants. All houses in the area were searched from time to time, often late at night when all its inhabitants could be expected to be at home. Simple details of age, occupation and personal characteristics were recorded on all inhabitants. Information was also collected on the layout of houses, furnishings and the colour of paint or wallpaper. All this information was brought together in local and central intelligence units and used to check answers given during routine screening sessions or more persistent questioning of suspects. Visiting journalists were sometimes asked to test the accuracy of the files by asking about the colour of the walls in a particular house which could then be searched to verify the Army's record.

Arrest for 'screening' was applied on a rather more selective basis. Anyone found out late at night or in a suspicious area or otherwise thought likely to be involved would be arrested, taken to the local Army intelligence centre and asked a number of routine questions on his or her identity, activities and associates. Questions might also be asked about recent terrorist incidents to see if any leads on those responsible could be obtained. Anyone thought to be in any way involved might be handed over to the police for more extended interrogation. The precise extent of Army intelligence involvement in the subsequent interrogation is unclear. The basic techniques of interrogation in depth, as will be seen, appear to have been developed by the Army and handed on to RUC Special Branch officers who were formally in control of extended questioning. But it seems likely that there was close and continuing involvement by Army intelligence not least because of the need for the Army to collect sufficient information to justify the internment of those suspects against whom sufficient admissible evidence of involvement in particular criminal offences to justify a prosecution could not be obtained. The Army in this period was required to produce at least three 'traces' pointing to the involvement of a suspect in the IRA before internment would be authorised.

The legality of some of these practices was doubtful. The Diplock Commission, which was established to review the need for emergency powers on the imposition of direct rule in 1972, recommended that the security forces should retain the power to search houses for arms and explosives and wanted persons, that the Army should have a power to detain any person suspected of being involved in or having knowledge of terrorist activities for four hours to establish his or her identity; but it was stressed that this proposal did not involve questioning 'directed to any other purpose than establishing the identity of the person arrested', and that any further arrest for questioning should be on specific grounds.[3] In the Northern Ireland (Emergency Provisions) Act 1973 the Army was given slightly different powers: to stop and question any person to establish his or her identity and to find out what he or she knows of terrorist incidents (s.16), and to arrest and detain for up to four hours any person suspected of criminal activity (s.12). The power to enter and search houses without warrant was specifically limited to the search for arms or explosives (s.13) or for the arrest of a person suspected of criminal activity (s.12(3)). It is clear that these powers did not justify large scale screening and house searches of the kind which were carried out prior to 1975. Figures for the use of the Army's power to arrest have never been regularly published. But the figures for house searches set out in Table 4.2 give some indication of the scale on which Army intelligence gathering was mounted. In 1973, for example, some 75,000 houses, almost one fifth of the total number of houses in Northern Ireland, were searched: in practice many fewer houses were searched much more frequently.

The abandonment of internment and the system of military intelligence on which it was based has resulted in a progressive curtailment of most of these activities. This is well illustrated in statistical terms by the very sharp decline in the number of house searches. Some mass house searching and headcounting is still continued, particularly in what are termed 'follow-up' operations in the aftermath of attacks on Army patrols. But large scale screening has been virtually abandoned. Most arrests for questioning are now carried out by the police or by joint Army/police patrols, and the questioning itself is wholly in the hands of the police. The principal task of the Army is now the maintenance of regular foot patrols, vehicle patrols, the manning of vehicle check points (VCPs) and the provision of bomb disposal units. But there has also been a substantial increase in undercover intelligence and surveillance operations. Much of this involves the use of new technological devices, such as concealed cameras, telephone tapping and a computerised data bank on the bulk of the population in Northern Ireland. There is no such immediate objective, however, for these operations as in the period when the Army was in a position to secure the internment of those identified by military intelligence as active terrorists.

There is a good deal of frustration in the Army over this curtailment of their operations, and their effective subordination to the police in respect of the processes of arrest and prosecution. This frustration in both operational and strategic terms has led on occasions to the development of alternative strategies for the 'elimination' of active terrorists. During 1978 the Army appear to have developed a policy of laying ambushes for suspected terrorists with a view to shooting dead those

Table 4.2: Official figures on house searches (including unoccupied houses)

1971	1972	1973	1974	1975	1976	1977	1978	1979
17262	36617	74556	71914	30092	34939	20724	15462	6452

Source: Northern Ireland Information Service.

Table 4.3: Persons shot dead by undercover Army patrols between December 1977 and November 1978

Colm McNutt	*IRSP member*	Shot in Londonderry on 12 December 1977; Army claim he was involved in a hijack attempt on an unmarked military patrol car; Republican sources allege he was shot on street without warning.
Paul Duffy	*Provisional IRA volunteer*	Shot on 26 February 1978 in Ardboe by patrol lying in wait at arms dump; Army claim he refused to surrender and was shot trying to escape; Republican sources allege he was shot without warning.
Denis Heaney	*Provisional IRA volunteer*	Shot in June 1978 in Londonderry; Army claim he was involved in a hijack attempt on an unmarked military patrol car; Republican sources allege that he was shot without warning, though they admit that he was on 'active service'.
James Mulvenna Denis Brown Jackie Mealy	*Provisional IRA volunteers*	All four men were shot in North Belfast on 21 June 1978 by an undercover Army patrol lying in wait at a bombing target; Army claim they were shot during gun battle; Republican sources allege that no arms were found, but admit that the three were on a bombing mission.
Billy Hanna	*Innocent passer-by*	
John Boyle	*Innocent teenager*	Shot by undercover patrol lying in wait at arms dump in cemetery; Army claim he was shot in error when he acted suspiciously when looking to see if the gun he had reported had been removed; soldiers charged with murder but acquitted.
James Taylor	*Innocent wildfowler*	Shot by undercover Army patrol near Coagh on 30 September 1978; Taylor's car tyres were let down and when he returned to scene with his uncle and asked for an explanation from soldiers in cars which had followed them, he was shot dead; Army later apologise for error.
Patrick Duffy	*Provisional IRA volunteer*	Shot by undercover patrol lying in wait at arms dump in Bogside, Londonderry on 25 November 1978; Army claim he was shot after picking up a gun; Republican sources allege he was shot without warning.

Source: Hibernia, *8 February 1979.*

who did not immediately give themselves up. In a series of incidents a number of alleged terrorists collecting arms or explosives or taking part in robberies or bombings were shot dead. But this approach caused more problems than it solved. Of the ten people shot dead in such operations between December 1977 and November 1978 three were admitted by the Army to have been shot in error (see Table 4.3). Since then the main pressure from the Army has been for the reintroduction of some form of 'selective' internment through which those identified by military intelligence as high level organisers or persistent hit men could be arrested and detained without the need to prove specific criminal activity.

The police

As the role of the Army as the primary agency in identifying and dealing with terrorists has declined, that of the police has gradually increased. In the period from 1971-5, as explained in *Law and State,* the RUC was largely excluded from effective operation in the main Catholic areas, with the result that police prosecutions were more likely to be brought against Loyalist than Republican suspects. Since 1975 there has been a deliberate policy of reintroducing RUC patrols in all areas, though regular foot patrols in West Belfast and Derry are still ruled out.

The differential pattern of deployment in Republican and Loyalist areas, however, is still observable in terms of arrest operations. In those cases in which the details were recorded, almost all Loyalist suspects were arrested by independent police action, while more than half the Republican suspects were arrested by Army patrols or joint Army/police patrols. A much higher proportion of Republican suspects were arrested in dawn patrols: at least two thirds of the Republican defendants covered in our survey were arrested between 1 am and 9 am compared with a figure of two fifths for Loyalists. This difference appears to have been due largely to perceived dangers in Republican areas, in which a daytime or evening arrest operation is more likely to spark off a confrontation with local people. There was much less difference between Loyalist and Republican defendants in terms of the precise legal power of arrest used. In almost all cases the security forces use their general power of arrest for questioning under the Northern Ireland (Emergency Provisions) Act 1978 or the Prevention of Terrorism (Temporary Provisions) Act 1976 in preference to their power to arrest suspects for specific criminal offences. This policy was openly admitted to the Bennett Committee:

> We have been informed by the RUC that it is their policy to arrest every terrorist suspect, even if caught in the act of committing a specific offence, under their powers either under section 11 of the 1978 Act or section 12 of the 1976 Act. One clear advantage to the

police of doing so is to give them more time in which to carry out their investigations.[4]

This policy has significant legal implications. In the first place the legal requirements for a valid arrest under the Northern Ireland (Emergency Provisions) Act 1978 are less demanding than those under the ordinary criminal law. The police officer need not specify to the defendant or have in mind any specific offence other than that the person arrested is a terrorist, which is broadly defined as 'a person who is or has been concerned in the commission or attempted commission of any act of terrorism or in directing, organising or training persons for the purpose of terrorism' (s.31); terrorism is defined as 'the use of violence for political ends and includes any use of violence for the purpose of putting the public or any section of the public in fear' (s.31). Nor is there any requirement under this provision that the suspicion need be reasonable. In the second place any person validly arrested under this power may be held for up to three days, and it is generally assumed that this authorises persistent questioning for that period. No regular figures for the use of this power are published. But the Bennett Committee revealed that in the period from September 1977 to August 1978 2,814 persons were arrested for questioning under the Emergency Provisions Act and the Prevention of Terrorism Act and that only one third were charged with specific offences.[5]

There is somewhat more formal protection for those arrested under the Prevention of Terrorism (Temporary Provisions) Act 1976.[6] The police officer must have a reasonable suspicion that the person to be arrested has been guilty of an offence under the Act or has been concerned in the commission, preparation or instigation of acts of terrorism (s.12). On the other hand, persons arrested under this power may be held for up to seven days. The requirement that ministerial approval be given for detention beyond 48 hours gives little practical protection, since ministers are merely informed that the police think there is good reason to hold the person for an extended period of questioning. In the period from November 1974 to September 1979 711 persons were arrested under the Prevention of Terrorism Act in Northern Ireland; ministerial approval for extended questioning was granted in 582 cases and refused in only two; yet only 327 (46%) of those arrested were charged with criminal offences.[7]

The combined effect of these provisions is to authorise what amounts to a 'trawling' operation among those thought likely to be in any way involved in terrorism or in an unlawful organisation. In our survey of cases tried early in 1979 there were numerous instances of the arrest and prolonged questioning of young Catholics. A number of them confessed to serious offences. But others confessed to no more than a brief period of membership of the Fianna, sometimes a number of years previously. And it must be remembered that our sample probably covered only one in three of those arrested and questioned. There is a strong case, as will be argued in greater detail below, for some more effective control over the use of the power to arrest for questioning if public confidence in the legitimacy of police powers and practice is to be restored in some Catholic areas. At the very least regular figures should be published on the use of the power to arrest under the Northern Ireland (Emergency Provisions) Act as they are under the Prevention of Terrorism Act.

In more general terms, however, the shift in the balance of power from the Army to the police does mean that arrests are now made primarily with a view to obtaining evidence for the prosecution of suspects rather than with a view to possible internment, which, in the view of the Bennett Committee, was the primary legislative purpose of the power to arrest any suspected terrorist under section 11 of the 1978 Act.[8] The significance of this change is perhaps best illustrated by the occasional conflict between the Army and the police in respect of the arrest by the Army of persons who are on the Army list of suspected persons, but who are not wanted by the police. The most notorious case in this respect has been that of Gerry Adams, the President of Provisional Sinn Fein, the political wing of the Provisional IRA, who was acquitted in a Diplock court of membership of the IRA in 1978, but who has been arrested on a number of subsequent occasions.[9]

Criminalisation

The practical significance of the abandonment of internment without trial in 1975 in terms of the relative roles of the Army and the police has been the curtailment of the system of military intelligence on which internment was based. But the change in policy has also been associated with an attempt to influence public perceptions of the nature of the conflict. Instead of accepting and attempting to deal with the IRA and its counterparts as overtly political forces the authorities have attempted to emphasise the criminality of their activities. The object of this exercise in labelling has been to assist in lessening whatever communal support there was for the various paramilitary groups.

There have been a number of interrelated aspects of this exercise. In the first place the government has consistently stressed that all suspected terrorists are now being dealt with under the ordinary criminal process, and that those who are imprisoned are convicted criminals. On a number of occasions the Northern Ireland Office has inserted full page advertisements in local newspapers listing the crimes for which those who have been claiming political status in the prisons have been convicted. In the second place the government made a deliberate and well publicised decision to phase out 'special category status' for those convicted of terrorist offences committed after March 1976. This special status had been granted to prisoners who were accepted as members of paramilitary organisations in 1972 following negotiations between government representatives and the Provisional IRA, and meant in practice that they were not required to work and wear prison clothes like ordinary criminals. Finally the government has repeatedly stressed that it will not enter into negotiations of any kind with illegal or paramilitary organisations.

There are a number of obvious difficulties facing the authorities in pursuing this policy of criminalisation. In the first place, those who are prosecuted for terrorist offences are *not* dealt with under the ordinary criminal law. Special provisions for arrest, questioning and trial have been enacted both under the Northern Ireland (Emergency Provisions) Act and the Prevention of Terrorism Act. These are described in detail in Chapters 5 and 6. But in general terms the fact that suspected terrorists are arrested under special powers and tried in special courts makes it easy for those who are convicted to deny that they are ordinary criminals. The continuing saga of the campaign both inside and outside the prisons for the granting of political status to IRA and other paramilitary prisoners is described in detail in Chapter 7. The most important difficulty, however, is that whether the authorities like it or not most offences committed by members of the IRA and other paramilitary organisations are in fact carried out with a deliberate political purpose, and that those who commit them do not regard themselves and are not generally regarded by the population at large as the same as ordinary criminals. It does not follow that the authorities are wrong to pursue a policy of dealing with those responsible for political violence by ordinary criminal procedures. But it is important, as we shall argue in Chapter 7, not to lose sight of the fact that there is a difference between ordinary criminals and those involved in the IRA campaign and in counter-operations on the Loyalist side.

Conclusion

The difference in Army and police roles in dealing with politically motivated violence, whether expressed as communal rioting or as terrorist attacks, should not be exaggerated. To a large extent the different functions which have been performed by the British Army and by the police are a matter of deployment. In the early period the police were excluded from active patrolling, riot control and even arrest operations in troubled Catholic areas. As the policy of Ulsterisation has been put into effect, the police have progressively taken over more and more of the tasks which from 1969 onwards were generally carried out by the Army. In doing so they have encountered some of the same difficulties which the Army has long faced in carrying out an effective policing operation without being drawn into the kind of confrontations and incidents which are likely to cause an escalation in communal antagonism or terrorist reprisals.

The problem arises in its starkest form over the use of guns by the security forces. Since 1969 there has been continuing concern and controversy over a series of incidents in which rioters and alleged terrorists have been killed or seriously injured by soldiers or policemen. We have already given details of ten such incidents in the period from December 1977 to November 1978, when the army appeared to have adopted a deliberate policy of shooting suspected terrorists. Since then there has not been such an obvious pattern of incidents. But the number of people who have been killed or seriously injured by Army and police patrols has remained high: there was only one such killing in 1979, but in the period from March to August 1980 there were as many as seven killings. In law the security forces are permitted to shoot to kill only where there is a direct and immediate threat to someone else's or their own lives. This is explained in some detail in the 'yellow card' issued to all soldiers. But there have been numerous incidents, notably those involving cars stolen by youngsters in West Belfast for what is called 'joy-riding', in which Army and police patrols have opened fire in circumstances in which there would not appear to have been any such direct or immediate threat.

In circumstances in which shooting and bombing attacks are regularly made on members of the security forces, it is understandable that soldiers and policemen should be tempted to use their own guns in any case in which they suspect that they may be about to be attacked with lethal weapons. If it can be shown that the use of firearms by members of the security forces was unreasonable in all the circumstances, those concerned are open to prosecution for murder or manslaughter. But few cases have been brought, and, in those which have, the defendants have all been acquitted, not least because the courts have clearly given defendants the benefit of any possible doubt.[10] As in respect of prosecutions for alleged ill-treatment during interrogation, discussed in Chapter 5, it seems clear that internal administrative controls on the use of firearms are more likely to prove effective in preventing abuse than the threat of possible prosecution.

The problem of shooting incidents is merely an example of the more general problem of ensuring that the security forces deal with riots and suspected terrorists with minimum necessary force. It cannot be over-emphasised how important this is to achieving a gradual return to normality, given the support which paramilitary organisations and the IRA in particular can gain from every abuse of power by the security forces. It is for this reason that it remains essential to stress the difference between a military and a civilian policing response to both rioting and terrorist activity. In the short-term there is a strong case for amending the terms of the powers granted to stop and search suspects

33

and to search houses to ensure that they are used only on the basis of reasonable suspicion that an offence has been committed or that arms or explosives have been hidden there. This applies particularly to the search of occupied houses at night, in respect of which we believe that a search warrant should be required in all cases other than those of hot pursuit.

In the longer term there is an equally strong case for emphasising the primacy of the police by speeding up the withdrawal of the Army from regular street patrolling and their replacement by more normal policing wherever possible. The aim should be to reduce the role of the Army to that of a garrison force, available in emergencies to deal with incidents in which full military force is required and to prevent any paramilitary body from asserting control over any area of the Province. In pursuing this strategy of withdrawal to barracks on the part of the Army, however, it is equally important to ensure that the police are not permitted to develop a paramilitary role. It is for this reason that internal controls over the use of firearms by the police are so important. The ultimate objective is to restore the confidence of the whole community in a police force which is committed to dealing with and, where possible, preventing the use of force for political purposes by relying on the ordinary rules and procedures of the criminal law.

5. INTERROGATION

The importance of intelligence on terrorist organisations and activities has been recognised since the start of the IRA campaign. The procedures and practice of questioning and interrogation have been at the centre of attention since 1971, when the first major series of allegations of torture and brutality during 'interrogation in depth' was made. We are not in a position − nor is anyone else − to give a definitive verdict on the truth of the continuing allegations that have been made between then and the present. The IRA has an obvious interest in exaggerating the extent of ill-treatment and the authorities in denying that it ever occurred. It is sufficient for our purposes that two official British inquiries have expressed their concern on practices current in 1971 and 1977, and that various allegations have been upheld both in the courts in Northern Ireland and by the European Commission and European Court of Human Rights.[1] The purpose of this chapter is not to review the evidence on the precise nature and extent of the malpractices that have occurred. It is to analyse the wider significance of the various practices of interrogation which have admittedly been developed and their relationship to more general concerns over the rights of suspects.

The common law rules on questioning

The right of the police at common law to question suspects has long been controversial. In strict law there is a right of silence in the sense that while the police may ask questions of anyone, whether a suspect or not, there is no obligation to answer them. Nor have the police any general power to arrest for questioning. Until 1898 an accused person was not even permitted to give evidence on the general ground that he could not be expected to tell the truth. In reality suspects have always been questioned, and confessions or admissions during questioning have long been the principal basis of convictions. The important legal issue is not so much the right to silence as the limits of legitimate questioning.

The most important of the rules which now govern the admissibility of confessions, and thus the legitimacy of any questioning leading to the confession, is that no statement by an accused person should be admitted as evidence unless it is wholly voluntary. There have been numerous judicial decisions on what constitutes a voluntary statement. Any form of physical violence or threat of violence will clearly render the statement involuntary, and in most cases would in addition constitute a separate criminal offence by those responsible. It is also clearly established that any form of inducement, for instance an offer of lenient treatment if the suspect confesses, will likewise make the confession involuntary. And in an important decision in the Northern Ireland Court of Appeal in 1968 it was held that a confession could not be held to be wholly voluntary if it was taken in circumstances which were designed to put pressure on the suspect to confess.[2]

This general principle has been supplemented by more detailed rules on the conduct of questioning. These were originally formulated by the judges in response to a request by the Chief Constable of Birmingham in 1912 for some guidance on what the courts would consider to be legitimate when deciding on the admissibility of confessions. They have been subsequently revised by the judges and supplemented by additional guidance from the Home Office. The current version, known as the Judges' Rules and Administrative Directions to the Police, makes it clear that any questioning should stop as soon as it becomes clear that the suspect is to be charged for a specific offence, and lays down precise rules for taking statements from such suspects.[3] The best known of these is the requirement that suspects should be formally cautioned and told that they need not say anything but that anything they do say will be taken down and may be used in evidence. But there are also explicit rules on the way in which suspects are to be treated while in a police station, on access to lawyers and on the position of juveniles. The version of the Judges' Rules and Administrative Directions to the Police which is currently applicable in Northern Ireland is that which was introduced in England in 1964. This version was introduced in Northern Ireland in place of the original rules only in 1976.

It is arguable how far these rules legitimate the kind of police questioning which is regularly carried out throughout the United Kingdom and other common law jurisdictions in connection with ordinary criminal activities. It is quite clear that they rule out many of the techniques of interrogation which have been developed in Northern Ireland and elsewhere. Interrogation in this sense is perhaps best defined as prolonged and persistent questioning in which the suspect's right to silence is implicitly if not formally denied. The development of techniques and procedures for such interrogation accordingly poses serious legal problems.

The development of interrogation in Northern Ireland

Prior to the outbreak of the troubles in 1969 the RUC do not appear to have acted very differently from other police forces in questioning suspects. As in all police forces a certain amount of violence was undoubtedly used. But there were few incidents of a kind to cause public concern. In the immediate aftermath of the internment operation in August 1971 allegations were made of systematic maltreatment of suspects during prolonged interrogation. The report of the Compton Committee in November 1971 confirmed that a selected number of suspects arrested in the internment operation had been subjected to what was called 'interrogation in depth' over periods of up to five days.[4] This involved subjecting the suspects to prolonged periods of interrogation interspersed with prolonged periods of wallstanding and other debilitating exercises; suspects were also deprived of food and sleep, hooded and exposed to continuous monotonous noise. There is little doubt that most were also subjected to repeated beatings though the precise extent of this was not established by the Compton Committee. The purpose of these 'five techniques', as they came to be called, was clearly to break down the resistance of the suspects so that they would reveal all that they knew of terrorist organisation and activity. They had been developed by the Army in its operations in Malaya, Kenya and Aden and appear to have been passed on to the RUC Special Branch, though the precise responsibility for their introduction has still not been clarified.[5]

In response to general public concern throughout Britain and elsewhere at the findings of the Compton Committee the government appointed a further committee, the Parker Committee, to report on the policy question of whether the use of these techniques could be justified.[6] The majority on the committee concluded that the techniques could be justified in the special circumstances then prevailing in Northern Ireland, and that since some at least of them were almost certainly unlawful legislation should be introduced to authorise their continued use. The government, however, were persuaded by the arguments in Lord Gardiner's minority report that such techniques were counter-productive and even if they were productive could not be justified. When the Parker Report was published in March 1972 it was announced by the Prime Minister that the five techniques would be abandoned.[7]

Despite the formal abandonment of the five techniques it is clear that prolonged interrogation of suspects was continued. Under the Civil Authorities (Special Powers) Act (Northern Ireland) 1922, the security forces had power to arrest and detain any person for up to 48 hours, and this power was widely used both for screening and for more sustained interrogation. There were also continuing complaints about the use of violence and threats of violence and on occasions of wallstanding and other similarly exhausting exercises. A number of complaints about ill-treatment of those being interrogated by the police at the Holywood

Army Barracks in the period from August to December 1971 were eventually found to be justified in proceedings before the European Commission on Human Rights.[8] Of more immediate practical significance, however, was the fact that the Northern Ireland judges continued to apply the established common law rules on the admissibility of confessions. During 1972 in a number of test cases the judges held that confessions obtained during prolonged interrogation were involuntary and therefore inadmissible. In *R. v. Flynn and Leonard* the Lord Chief Justice described the detention centre at Holywood as 'a set-up officially organised and operated to obtain information . . . from persons who would otherwise have been less than willing to give it', he went on to say that in general 'admissions made by persons under this type of interrogation in this setting will often fail to qualify as voluntary statements'.[9] A substantial number of other prosecutions were abandoned by the Director of Public Prosecutions on the ground that confessions obtained in such circumstances were unlikely to be held admissible.[10]

This turn of events was not welcomed by the security authorities who were under pressure to deal with as many suspects as possible by criminal prosecutions as opposed to internment without trial. Their concern was shared by the Diplock Commission set up in the aftermath of the imposition of direct rule in 1972 to review the legal procedures for dealing with terrorists:

> We consider that the detailed technical rules and practice as to the 'admissibility' of inculpatory statements by the accused as they are currently applied in Northern Ireland are hampering the course of justice in the case of terrorist crimes and compelling the authorities responsible for public order and safety to resort to detention in a significant number of cases which could otherwise be dealt with both effectively and fairly by trial in a court of law.[11]

The Diplock Commission accordingly recommended that the law should be changed to allow statements obtained in breach of the common law rules to be admitted in evidence provided that they could not be shown to have been obtained by subjecting the accused to torture or to inhuman or degrading treatment.[12] This recommendation was duly adopted under the Northern Ireland (Emergency Provisions) Act 1973. It was clearly intended, in combination with the new power for the police to arrest and detain suspects for questioning for up to 72 hours, to give legislative authority for the continued use of prolonged interrogation, which in the words of the Diplock Committee is designed 'to build up an atmosphere in which the initial desire to remain silent is replaced by an urge to confide in the questioner'.[13] The period for which suspects could be held was further extended in 1974 under the Prevention of Terrorism (Temporary Provisions) Act 1974 which gave the police throughout the UK the power to hold suspects for questioning for up to 48 hours and with the formal consent of the Home Secretary or Secretary of State for Northern Ireland for a further five days.[14]

These provisions did not assume major significance until the ending of internment in 1975. From then there was increasing pressure on the police to secure the conviction of suspected terrorists. Given the difficulty of obtaining independent evidence in the majority of cases this meant in practice that confessions had to be obtained. A decision was made to construct two special interrogation centres, one in Castlereagh in Belfast and the other at Gough Army Barracks in Armagh.[15] Both were designed in such a way as to increase the sense of isolation of those held there in that neither cells nor interview rooms had any windows. The opening of these new centres at Castlereagh early in 1977 and at Gough in November 1977 coincided with a major increase in the number of complaints against the police in respect of ill-treatment during interrogation. The number of such complaints increased from 180 in 1975 to 384 in 1976 and 671 in 1977.[16] At the same time there was increasing concern both from police doctors and from external pressure groups about the techniques being used in these centres. From April 1977 repeated formal representations were made by the Association of Forensic Medical Officers about the number of suspects who showed signs of physical maltreatment during and after their interrogations at Castlereagh. Similar representations were made by the police surgeons at Gough early in 1978. In November 1977 an investigation was carried out by a special team from Amnesty International of a number of cases of alleged ill-treatment. Their report calling for a public inquiry was submitted to the British Government in May 1978[17] and was followed shortly after by the appointment of the Bennett Committee on Police Interrogation Procedures in Northern Ireland. The Bennett Committee was not empowered to investigate individual allegations but made it clear in its report in March 1979 that it accepted that there had been cases 'in which injuries whatever their precise cause had not been self-inflicted and had been sustained in police custody'.[18] It accordingly made a series of recommendations designed to improve the supervision of interrogation and to eliminate the possibility of further abuses. In particular it recommended that closed circuit television should be installed in all interview rooms and monitored by uniformed branch officers, that the number of detective officers interviewing any one suspect should be limited to two at a time and not more than six in all, that interrogation should not continue through meal-breaks or continue after midnight, except for urgent operational reasons, that all suspects should have an absolute right of access to their solicitor after 48 hours in custody, and that a formal code of conduct for interviewing officers should be incorporated in the RUC Code. These recommendations were eventually accepted by the government in

June 1979.[19]

Little purpose would now be served by reviewing in detail the evidence on the extent and nature of the abuses which undoubtedly occurred during interrogation by the RUC in this period. The underlying cause of the rapid increase in the number of complaints in 1976 and 1977 was probably the pressure put on the police by the Northern Ireland Secretary, Roy Mason, to obtain convictions and the failure of ministers and senior officers in the RUC to make it clear that malpractices during interrogation would not be tolerated. In these circumstances it was natural for interviewing officers to assume that the authorities were more interested in the number of confessions obtained than in the methods used to obtain them. The procedures for dealing with complaints against the police were also seriously deficient, as discussed below. Following the report of the Bennett Committee and the appointment of a new Chief Constable in 1980 the level of complaint has dropped sharply. But there are certain aspects of the interrogation system which have not been affected by the recommendations of the Bennett Committee and which have equally important long term implications. Our account of interrogation practice during the period of our survey is directed primarily at these broader issues.

Interrogation practice in 1977 and 1978

Our information on practice in interrogation is taken from the court files of those defendants who came before the courts in the period of our survey. These files contained brief details of the dates and times of arrest and interrogation of each suspect. There are some obvious dangers in relying on this data. In the first place the accuracy of police records cannot be guaranteed. In a number of cases the list of interrogation sessions was almost certainly incomplete and in a few it may have been inaccurate. On the other hand we have no reason to believe that the records were systematically falsified. In the second place the information related only to those who were actually prosecuted as a result of their interrogation. The Bennett Committee revealed that only one third (35%) of those held for questioning between September 1977 and August 1978 were charged with criminal offences.[20] Our sample was thus limited to a similar proportion of those arrested and interrogated and includes only those cases in which a confession was made or other admissible evidence was available. In the third place most of those covered in our survey were arrested and interrogated in the early part of 1978, that is before the introduction of the various reforms recommended by the Bennett Committee. Finally the court files did not contain details of the defence case or of the grounds on which a confession may have been contested at the eventual trial. Despite all these deficiencies, however, we are satisfied that the information was generally reliable and that it provided a fairly accurate picture of practice in interrogation at that time.

In a typical case the process would begin with a dawn arrest by a police or joint Army/police patrol. The suspect would then be taken either to a local police station or direct to one of the main interrogation centres. There he would be medically examined and allocated to a cell by uniformed police officers pending the start of interrogation. The first interrogation session would be unlikely to take place much before noon. But from then until late that night the suspect would be interrogated by two or three teams of detectives in continuous sessions of up to two hours. In some cases a new team of detectives would take over without any effective break in the interrogation, so that from the suspect's point of view the session might last for three or four hours. A similar pattern of interviews would be held the following day, starting about 10 am and continuing again until 10 or 11 pm. In the case of those arrested under the three-day power the series of interviews would be likely to come to an end in the late morning or early afternoon of the third day, when the suspect would be taken to an appropriate police station for formal charging. In the case of those arrested and held under the Prevention of Terrorism Act the series of interrogations might continue for five or six days.

This pattern of interrogation may be illustrated by two fairly typical cases, one in which the arrest and interrogation was under the three-day power and the other under the seven-day power.

A 24-year-old Republican was arrested at 4.55 am on 7 August 1978 and taken to an interrogation centre. Interrogation sessions were recorded over the next three days as follows:

7 August	11.00–13.15
	13.35–17.00
	17.35–19.15
	21.45–23.40
8 August	10.10–12.10
	14.00–15.55
	19.35–20.05
9 August	10.55–11.45

The suspect made statements admitting membership of the IRA and assisting in knee-capping operations at 15.20 on 8 August and 11.10 on 9 August and was charged with membership of an illegal organisation at 16.35 on 9 August.

A 24-year-old Loyalist was arrested at 6.00 am on 14 November 1977 and taken to an interrogation centre. Interrogation sessions were recorded over the next five days as follows:

14 November	11.35–12.50
	15.00–16.15
	16.15–17.05
15 November	10.30–11.40
	11.40–12.55
	14.15–15.25
	20.25–22.30
16 November	9.35–10.30
	11.00–12.40
	14.10–15.00
	15.40–16.50
	20.25–21.50
	22.00–23.20
17 November	10.20–11.40
	11.55–13.00
	13.15–14.05
	14.20–15.35
18 November	10.55–12.45

The suspect made statements on 16 November at 15.45, 20.45 and 22.10,

41

and on 17 November at 10.30, 12.05, 13.20 and 14.40; he was charged at 15.00 on 18 November on various counts of murder and bombing and membership of an illegal organisation.

In these examples, as in many other cases, the usual practice was followed of first obtaining an oral admission to a specific criminal offence and then asking the suspect to make a written statement in a subsequent session.

The overall picture is further clarified by the statistical analysis in Table 5.1. This shows that the majority of defendants spent between four and twelve hours in the interviewing room split into between four and nine separate sessions. The average length of time spent under interrogation was eight hours split into eight separate sessions. But there was a wide variation in the intensity of interrogation. One-third of the defendants were subjected to three or fewer sessions and one in five spent less than four hours under interrogation. But one in ten spent more than 16 hours under interrogation and one particular suspect was interrogated for a total of 41 hours. There was some difference in the treatment of Loyalist and Republican defendants. There was a tendency for rather more Loyalists to be interrogated for shorter periods and fewer sessions. But roughly equal proportions of the Loyalists and the Republicans were subjected to high-intensity interrogation for very long periods.

Table 5.1: The interrogation of defendants dealt with in Diplock Courts between January and April 1979

a. Number of sessions

	1-3	4-9	10 or more	NK
Loyalists (89)	39%	43%	12%	6%
Republicans (240)	27%	59%	9%	4%
Total (332)*	31%	54%	10%	5%

b. Total hours under interrogation

	Up to 4	4-9	10 or more	NK
Loyalists (89)	30%	29%	32%	9%
Republicans (240)	15%	45%	36%	5%
Total (332)*	19%	40%	33%	7%

*including three cases not identified as Loyalist or Republican.

The precise content and pattern of interrogation obviously depends on the response of the suspect. In cases where the suspect had been arrested on the basis of information connecting him with a specific incident, the questioning was likely to focus on that incident from the start. The detectives would probably start by asking for an account of his movements at the time in question and would then gradually reveal

42

the extent of the evidence against him. For instance, in one case the suspect was first told that 'his fingerprints had been found on the vehicle and they believed he was one of the people involved' and then later that one of his alleged accomplices had confessed. In cases where the arrest had been made on the basis of more general information suggesting that the suspect had been involved, the initial questioning was more likely to focus on general matters such as the suspect's associates and political views until some more specific information emerged. This approach was adopted in a substantial number of cases in our sample in which teenage Republicans were arrested and interrogated about alleged membership of the Fianna or the IRA. In some cases of this kind the recorded notes of the questioning included lengthy discussions on how someone in the suspect's home area could avoid some kind of involvement in unlawful activities until an admission was obtained that the suspect had taken part in a riot or hijacking incident, often several years before, which would then be pursued in greater depth, particularly if the incident could be identified from police records. In others the suspect was recorded as having agreed to confess in response to being told for instance that the police 'had certain information which led them to believe he was a member of the Fianna'. In other cases it was simply recorded that the suspect confessed after sustained questioning: 'after continually questioning him for about half an hour he admitted he was a member of C Company Fianna from Christmas 1976'.

In almost every case it was the practice of the detectives to obtain an oral admission of an offence in the first place. This was generally recorded in the form of notes of 'question and answer' sessions. The suspect would then be asked to make a formal written statement in the next session. This statement was almost always written down by the detectives rather than by the suspect himself. Various reasons for this were recorded. The suspect was often said to have asked the detectives to write the statement for him, for instance on the grounds that 'he couldn't write very well' or that 'he was not a very good writer' or that 'youse know it all'. Given that the police already know the basic details of most incidents from the evidence of victims or other witnesses, it would not be hard for them to construct a fairly convincing confession without much further assistance from the suspect than his general agreement to sign. In some cases detectives also used the technique of getting the suspect to sign a sketch map of the incident. The probative value of such a map is of course minimal. But the production of such 'original' documents lend some verisimilitude to confessions written by the police. It is equally easy for detectives to implicate a suspect more deeply in a particular incident by the use of words which have a significant legal implication.

There was also some evidence from our sample of the use of inducements to obtain confessions contrary to the Judges' Rules. In one case where there was ample independent evidence of guilt, the suspects were not only subjected to extended interrogation but were induced to confess by the wholly improper threat that if they did not their mothers would be interviewed and then prosecuted if they gave a false alibi.

The efficacy of interrogation

It is easier to describe these techniques than to assess their efficacy. At one level they may be thought to be relatively successful. As shown in Table 5.2, in almost all the cases covered in our survey (86%) the defendant had made a confession. In a third of the cases (30%) this was supplemented by additional forensic or identification evidence which pointed to the guilt of the accused, but this additional evidence would often not have been sufficient to justify a conviction on its own.

Table 5.2: The nature of the evidence against defendants in Diplock trials between January and April 1979

	Statement only	Statement and other evidence	No statement	NK
Loyalists (89)	55%	35%	2%	7%
Republicans (240)	57%	29%	7%	7%
Total (332)*	56%	30%	6%	7%

*including three cases not identified as Loyalist or Republican.

The process of interrogation was also relatively successful in providing information for the security forces on other suspects. In a number of cases the record of question and answer sessions indicated that suspects had given the names of other persons involved in specific incidents or in general terrorist activity, though it was usual for this information to be excluded at the request of the suspect from any written statement. This tacit agreement that there should be 'no names' in any formal confession was clearly designed to reduce the fears of suspects that they would be punished by their colleagues on release.

This level of efficacy must be set against some other less attractive aspects of the system. In the first place, those who confessed probably represented only about one-third of those subjected to prolonged interrogation. The figures released by the Bennett Committee for the period between September 1977 and August 1978 showed that only 37% of those interrogated at Castlereagh and 24% of those interrogated at Gough and Strand Road, Londonderry were charged.[21] It follows either that very large numbers of innocent people were being subjected to prolonged interrogation or that prolonged interrogation failed to produce a confession from those who had something to confess in a substantial proportion of cases.

Concern on this issue is heightened by the fact that the large majority

44

of those who did make a confession did so relatively quickly. As shown in Table 5.3, half of those covered in our survey made their first statement within the first three hours of interrogation, and a further quarter within the next three hours. The number of further first confessions dropped off sharply after that point. In a large number of cases, however, an initial statement was followed by a series of other statements giving further details about the same incident or admissions about further incidents. It appears to have been the policy of detectives to break down suspects' admissions into a number of separate statements each relating to a number of discrete incidents, probably in order to avoid subsequent difficulties in the courts in cases in which a number of different defendants have to be dealt with together. This practice explains in part the fact that even those who made a statement early on their first day of interrogation were regularly held for the full three day period. Detectives were also clearly using further interrogation sessions as a means of eliciting from co-operative suspects as much information as they could about general terrorist organisation and activities in the suspect's home area. Nonetheless, the analysis in Table 5.3 must raise some doubt on the justification for holding and interrogating suspects for as long as three days.

Similar doubts must be raised by the growing body of psychological research into interrogation techniques.[22] The purpose of modern interrogation, as was made clear by the Diplock Committee, is to break the suspect's will to resist and to induce him to co-operate with his interrogators. This can often be achieved, according to the psychological evidence, in a relatively short time by isolating the suspect from all contacts which would strengthen his will to resist, by increasing the level of stress and fatigue and by creating a general sense of uncertainty. Some psychologists, notably William Sargant, have compared this process to the experimental neurosis produced by Pavlov in some of his dogs by varying positive and negative rewards for certain actions.[23] Whatever the scientific explanation, it is clear that the conditions at Castlereagh and Gough Barracks, and to a lesser extent in other police stations, approximate closely to those generally regarded as likely to 'break' even the strongest wills. The suspect is isolated for at least three and perhaps up to seven days from all contact other than with his

Table 5.3: Total number of hours of interrogation before first statement by defendants in Diplock trials between January and April 1979

	Less than 1 hour	1-2 hours	2-3 hours	3-6 hours	7-9 hours	10 or more hours	No state-ment	NK
Loyalists (89)	13%	22%	17%	21%	7%	4%	2%	12%
Republicans (240)	7%	22%	20%	25%	5%	7%	7%	6%
Total (332)*	9%	22%	19%	23%	6%	6%	6%	8%

*including three cases not identified as Loyalist or Republican.

interrogators and gaolers. He experiences obvious stress, both from his natural fears about possible long-term imprisonment and from the widespread stories about beatings and torture inflicted on some suspects. He is likely to suffer increasing fatigue, not least from having been kept awake from very early in the morning of his initial arrest until late that night and from the difficulty of sleeping in such a strange environment. And he must face a long series of interviews with two or three teams of detectives who may well alternate their tactics to appear sometimes friendly and sometimes threatening. Even if there is no physical violence, the likelihood that suspects will do anything to please their captors, including making a false confession, clearly increases with the length of time they are required to undergo these combined pressures. Many of those released from Castlereagh and other interrogation centres have given convincing accounts of the sense of disorientation they have experienced. Even in the police records of interrogations there are occasional references to the difficulty that a suspect will have in 'holding out' for the full period of his detention as a ground for making an early confession. Some of those held under the Prevention of Terrorism Act were clearly threatened with having to undergo the full seven day period if they did not co-operate.

The use of pressures of this kind might perhaps be thought by some to be justifiable if they helped to bring to justice those responsible for serious terrorist offences. The danger is that they may also result in false confessions. It has been established beyond reasonable doubt that there have been a number of wrongful convictions in Britain based on apparently voluntary confessions, as for instance in the Maxwell Confait case.[24] There are no cases in Northern Ireland where it has been so clearly established that someone has been wrongly convicted on the basis of a false confession. But there have been a substantial number of cases in which serious doubts have been raised about the validity of confessions induced by prolonged interrogation. There is also the more general problem that the use of the techniques described above, even if there is no question of unlawful threats or violence, is likely to lessen general public confidence in the administration of justice.

There are two basic approaches to resolving these problems. The first is to attempt to create procedures and sanctions which will effectively eliminate any abuse during prolonged interrogation. The second is to prohibit it as inherently unacceptable and to create alternative methods by which those suspected of serious crimes may be brought to justice. In Northern Ireland the authorities have chosen the first alternative on the general grounds that the security forces must be permitted to arrest and interrogate those suspected of serious terrorist offences. Since this general strategy is unlikely to be changed in the immediate future we shall first outline the deficiencies in the methods currently employed to reduce the possibility of abuse during interrogation and suggest some ways in which they might be improved. But we shall also discuss some of the possible alternatives to the prolonged interrogation or questioning which is increasingly being employed by police forces throughout Britain.

The control of abuse

There are three potential controls on abuses during interrogation: the exclusion of a statement or confession obtained by improper means as evidence at the suspect's trial, the possible prosecution of detectives shown to be guilty of unlawful conduct, and internal administrative and disciplinary controls within the police. In Northern Ireland the first of these controls has been substantially weakened by the terms of the Northern Ireland (Emergency Provisions) Act and the second and third have until recently been shown to be largely ineffective.

The intention of the Diplock Commission in recommending what is now section 8 of the Northern Ireland (Emergency Provisions) Act 1978 was clearly to authorise the admission of statements obtained in breach of the common law rules. It is rather less clear how far beyond these rules it was intended that interrogators might go. Section 8 permits the admission of confessions obtained by any treatment short of torture or inhuman or degrading treatment under the terms of the European Convention on Human Rights, which has been held not to include occasional rough treatment or slaps about the head.[25] The judges in Northern Ireland, however, have consistently maintained that the terms of the section do not interfere with the residual discretion of the judge in a Diplock trial to exclude a statement even if there has not been torture or inhuman or degrading treatment. On the other hand the judges have felt bound to pay some attention to the purpose of the legislature in introducing section 8, and have accordingly applied less strict rules on admissibility than they did before the section came into force.

This was made very clear in the judgement of Lord Justice McGonigal in R. v. McCormick:[26]

Treatment to come within Article 3 (of the European Convention) must be treatment of a gross nature. It appears to accept a degree of physical violence which could never be tolerated by the courts under the common law test, and if the words in (section 8) are to be construed in the same sense as the words used in Article 3, it leaves open to an interviewer to use a moderate degree of physical mal-treatment for the purpose of inducing a person to make a statement. It appears to me that this is the way the words must be construed and that that is the effect of the section.

Despite this clear statement of the possible application of the section, the judge used his discretion to exclude a statement which in his view had been obtained by physical violence:

> That does not mean however that these courts will tolerate or permit physical maltreatment of a lesser degree deliberately carried out for the purpose of or which has the effect of inducing a person interviewed to make a statement. Not only would such conduct amount to an assault and in itself be an offence under the ordinary criminal law but it would be repugnant to all principles of justice to allow such conduct to be used as a means towards an end, however desirable that end might be made to appear.

But he added that the terms of section 8 must be given *some* effect:

> The effect of the exercise of the discretion if unfettered by the existence of (section 8) might be, therefore, to negative the effect of (section 8) and under the guise of the discretionary power have the effect of reinstating the old common law test insofar as it depended on the proof of physical or mental maltreatment . . . It should only be exercised in such cases where failure to exercise it might create injustice by admitting a statement which though admissible under the section and relevant on its face was *in itself* . . . suspect by reason of the method by which it was obtained, and by that I do not mean only a method designed and adopted for the purpose of obtaining it, but a method as a result of which it was obtained.

These lengthy quotations from what is now the leading case on the interpretation of section 8 have been given to illustrate the complexity of the reasoning which the judges have applied in their approach to contested confessions. In practice contested confessions have been excluded mainly where the judge has been satisfied by the medical evidence that there has been physical maltreatment and that that maltreatment was used in order to obtain a confession, that is that it was used by detectives before the confession was made. There have been a substantial number of such cases. The Bennett Committee reported that in the period between July 1976 and June 1978 15 confessions were held inadmissible in Diplock trials and a further 11 confessions were regarded as sufficiently suspect by the Director of Public Prosecutions for him not to proceed with a prosecution.[27] There were also a number of such cases during the period of our survey. It can hardly be doubted therefore, that the possible exclusion of statements did not act as an effective control of police malpractice. It may even be that the very wide terms of section 8 and the somewhat equivocal approach by the judges, not least in the McCormick case, led some interrogators to believe that the 'robust questioning' said by the judge to be permissible could be taken to include some degree of physical maltreatment.[28]

There has also been continuing uncertainty over the effect of section

48

8 on the admissibility of statements obtained in circumstances which constitute a breach of the Judges' Rules but without any question of violence or threats. There has been no clear ruling by the courts on whether or not the Judges' Rules apply to interrogation in custody. The most frequently used power of arrest under section 11 of the Northern Ireland (Emergency Provisions) Act 1978 authorises the arrest of suspected terrorists. There is no requirement that the police should suspect those arrested of any particular offence. The power granted under section 11 is in effect a power to arrest for questioning. It is thus arguable that the Judges' Rules do not apply since they assume that suspects are arrested only on suspicion of particular offences.

In their discussion of this problem the Bennett Committee referred to the fact that the RUC Code requires any statement obtained during an interview which is to be used in criminal proceedings to be taken in accordance with legal requirements and the Judges' Rules.[29] It appears to have been assumed by those concerned that this requirement applied only to interviews carried out for the purpose of obtaining evidence on specific charges and not to interviews which were primarily devoted to intelligence gathering. There was no indication in the cases we studied that this distinction was maintained in practice. When written statements were obtained the forms and cautions prescribed in the Judges' Rules appear to have been used. But there was ample evidence of breaches of the Judges' Rules in the process of questioning, in that charges were delayed and questioning continued long after clear admissions of guilt had been made. There were also some examples in the written records of questioning of improper threats or inducements.

We are not aware of any case in which a statement has been held to be inadmissible merely on the ground of such breaches of the Judges' Rules. In a few cases judges have used their residual discretion to exclude statements obtained by trickery or other improper practices. In one case in our sample the judge excluded an oral admission obtained from a defendant by a false claim by the detectives that 'they had ample evidence against him' and that there was a witness who could identify him, and after an assurance that what he said would not be written down and used in evidence; as there was no other evidence against him the defendant was acquitted.[30] In another trial in December 1979 the judge admitted a statement made by a 15-year-old schoolboy who was attending a school for the mentally handicapped at the time of the interview, and who was assessed as having the mental age of a child of eight, though it was accepted that the administrative direction requiring the presence of a parent or relative in such a case had not been complied with.[31] It appears to be generally assumed both by the police and by judges that many of the provisions of the Judges' Rules have been rendered inoperative by the terms of the Northern Ireland (Emergency Provisions) Act.

The formal procedure under which suspects may make a complaint against the police officers whom he alleges have illtreated him is equally ineffective. In theory all such complaints are reviewed by an independent body established in 1977, the Police Complaints Board. But the Board's role is confined to the consideration of possible disciplinary action as opposed to criminal proceedings. The so-called 'double jeopardy' rule, which is designed to protect police officers from facing both a prosecution and internal disciplinary sanctions for the same offence, further reduces the effective role of the Board, particularly since the rule is applied to all cases in which an allegation is referred to the Director of Public Prosecutions, even if no prosecution is ordered.[32] As a matter of practice all cases involving a complaint about treatment during interrogation are referred to the Director but only a handful result in a prosecution. In 1978 more than 1000 complaints files, covering all police activities, were submitted to the Director. In the 826 cases in which a decision was made the Director ordered that no proceedings be instituted against the police officers concerned in no less than 787 cases (97%).[33] None of these cases can be reopened by the Police Complaints Board unless a disciplinary offence separate from the allegation of criminal conduct can be identified.

Even if a prosecution is ordered against the police officers, a conviction is unlikely to be obtained. The Bennett Committee reported that no final conviction had been recorded in any case arising out of a complaint of illtreatment during interrogation up to the end of 1978.[34] Our own study likewise revealed a 100% acquittal rate in such cases. Given the conclusions of the Amnesty Report and of the Bennett Committee and the substantial number of cases in which judges have refused to admit confessions it is impossible to accept the argument that all complaints about illtreatment during interrogation have thus been shown to be unfounded. The underlying explanation for the decisions of the Director of Public Prosecutions and the courts is probably a mixture of the notorious reluctance of members of a closed organisation like the police force to give evidence against their colleagues and the very high standard of proof which is required to justify a prosecution or conviction against a member of the security forces.

Though the Bennett Committee recommended some minor changes in procedure to strengthen the existing complaints system, it clearly took the view that internal administrative controls within the police were the best protection against abuses during interrogation. It accordingly recommended more effective training and supervision of interrogation officers, the monitoring of all interviews by closed circuit television and the introduction of a specific section in the formal RUC Code on conduct during interrogation.[35] Almost all these recommendations were accepted in principle by the government in June 1979 and are currently being implemented. The recommendation that all persons being held for interrogation should have an unconditional right of access to their legal advisers after 48 hours, however, has only been partially accepted, in that the government insisted that the police should have a right to be present during any such interview, a condition that has proved unacceptable to most lawyers.[36]

We share the view of the Bennett Committee that internal supervision and internal sanctions are potentially the most effective means of controlling possible abuse during interrogation. Given the clear lack of commitment on these matters by some senior officers in the period from 1977 to 1979, however, we are not convinced that internal controls are sufficient. If the security forces are to retain the power to hold suspects for interrogation for as long as three days, some more formal legal control is necessary to protect suspects against a change of policy within the security forces. One method of achieving this aim — which would, in our view, best meet the need — would be the enactment of a statutory code of practice for the conduct of interrogations.

This would need to contain explicit provisions on the following matters:

i. the medical examination of suspects before, during and after interrogation;
ii. the limitation of interrogation sessions to four hours per day in sessions of not more than our hour each without a break for refreshment;
iii. a limited daily right of access for the suspect's relatives while the suspect is not undergoing interrogation, an unconditional right of access for his own doctor or a doctor nominated by him, and an unconditional right of access for his legal adviser after the first twenty-four hours of detention;
iv. a requirement that all juveniles and persons with subnormal intelligence should be interrogated in the presence of a parent or guardian;
v. the maintenance of a detailed formal record of arrest, medical examination, medication, interrogation sessions, meals, visits and complaints in respect of each suspect; a copy of this record should be available as of right to any person with a legitimate interest;
vi. a clear statement of the applicability of the general principle that confessions must not be obtained by force, threats or inducements.

A draft of a possible statutory code of interrogation practice along these lines is given in the Appendix.

The terms of this code should be enforceable by ordinary legal means, that is by an action for damages or an injunction. In addition any confession or statement obtained during interrogation should be admissible in evidence only if it is shown that the terms of the statutory code of practice have been adhered to. Section 8 of the Northern Ireland (Emergency Provisions) Act 1978 should be repealed and replaced accordingly. Finally, to ensure that internal disciplinary sanctions are duly applied, the independent Police Complaints Board should be required to consider the imposition of suitable disciplinary sanctions, including dismissal, demotion or removal from interrogation work, in all cases where a *prima facie* case of a breach of the code is established or in which a court holds a statement or confession to be inadmissible on the grounds of such a breach.

Should interrogation be normalised?

These suggestions for the regulation of interrogation have been made with a view to preventing some of the more obvious dangers of prolonged interrogation which have been identified by psychologists or highlighted by practice in Northern Ireland and elsewhere. Some further attention must also be given to the more significant and general issue of whether interrogation should be accepted as a normal method of dealing with serious crime. Provision for prolonged interrogation is an integral part of the current emergency legislation both in Britain and Northern Ireland. But there is little doubt that similar techniques are being used by police forces in Britain in cases which do not fall under the terms of the Prevention of Terrorism Act. There is considerable pressure from some leading politicians and policemen for this practice to be legalised by the enactment of a general right to arrest and hold for questioning persons suspected of serious offences. There is similar pressure for the removal of the so-called right to silence, so that suspects who fail to give an acceptable and convincing account of themselves in response to such questioning could be convicted even if there is not sufficient independent evidence to justify it.

The current position in Britain, as outlined above, is that under the Judges' Rules further questioning of a suspect is not permissible once the police have sufficient evidence to justify a charge. Nor is there any general legal authority to arrest a suspect and hold him for questioning. The reality of police practice is entirely different. Suspects for all kinds of offences are regularly taken to police stations and questioned for long periods. In such cases the police make a point of stressing that the suspect has agreed to 'come along to the station' and that he is merely 'helping the police with their inquiries'. The point of using this terminology is that it avoids possible problems over the legality of the questioning, since if the suspect is formally arrested it is arguable that the police must already have sufficient evidence to justify a charge and should not therefore be permitted to ask further questions. But it is widely recognised that if a suspect refused to go along to the station or tried to leave before the questioning had been completed he would in most cases be arrested. There is also a widespread practice of arresting suspects on a minor 'holding charge' and then questioning them while in police custody on the major offences for which they have in reality been taken in. The fundamental legal issue in this context is whether it is better to recognise the reality of police practice and to regulate it than to cling to the legal pretence that suspects are not held for questioning and that they are permitted to enjoy the right to silence.

The contribution which we can make to this general debate on the basis of our study of practice in interrogation in Northern Ireland is clearly limited. But the account which we have given of how the right to interrogate is used may assist in identifying the dangers in granting the police an unrestricted right to arrest for questioning. It may also assist in identifying some of the possible intermediate positions between an absolute right of silence and unrestricted interrogation.

Some of the more practical steps on the range of possibilities may perhaps be listed as follows:

i. an absolute right to silence, in the sense that no questioning of any kind would be permitted once a suspect has been taken to a police station;

ii. a requirement that a person reasonably suspected of an offence should submit to questioning, though without any obligation to answer;

iii. a requirement that a person reasonably suspected of an offence should be expected to give an explanation of his conduct, with the sanction that if he does not that may be used as evidence against him;

iv. a requirement that a person reasonably suspected of an offence be required to answer relevant questions with the sanction that failure to do so would in itself be an offence;

v. a formal right for the police to arrest and question for a specified period any person reasonably suspected of a serious offence.

All these levels, it should be noted, have already been adopted for particular purposes under British law. There is in law a more or less absolute right to silence in respect of most offences, and questioning by the police is in theory strictly limited by the Judges' Rules. There are other offences, however, notably the possession of stolen goods or offensive weapons, in respect of which a person found in possession is required to give an explanation if he wishes to avoid an inference of guilt.[37] There is also a requirement under the Bankruptcy and Companies Acts that persons suspected of certain malpractices should answer questions put to them.[38] Finally arrest for questioning by the police is implicitly authorised by the Prevention of Terrorism Act and is currently under consideration in the Criminal Justice (Scotland) Bill.[39] The important issue is not so much whether any of the levels is inherently undesirable, but which level should be adopted for general purposes.

Our own view, in the light of experience in Northern Ireland, is that any general power to arrest for questioning would be open to serious abuse. It might be used on a widespread, almost random, basis in areas where crime rates were high, as the Army's power to arrest for identification was used in Catholic areas in Northern Ireland. Furthermore, even if there were no physical violence or threats, it is clear that very substantial psychological pressure and stress could be put on those who were isolated and kept in custody for questioning even for relatively short periods. And it is difficult in practical terms to eliminate the risk of threats or ill-treatment, or to establish conclusively whether or not they occurred, given the natural interest on the part of suspects to allege that any admission was improperly obtained and on the part of the police to deny it.

Some of these possible abuses might be controlled. Provision for the tape-recording and video-taping of all interviews would help to reduce the risk of most forms of improper pressure during questioning. Strict limitation of the length of time for which a suspect might be held, and of the duration of questioning sessions would help to reduce the risks of prolonged isolation and stress. A requirement that any confession obtained by any means which constituted a breach of the Judges' Rules should require corroboration, as recommended in the Fisher Report,[40] would likewise help to reduce the risk of conviction on the basis of an unsound confession.

The main argument against granting the police a power to arrest for questioning, subject to stringent safeguards of this kind, is that it would further consolidate the shift in the focus of attention in the trial of serious offences from the courtroom to the police station. In practice it would amount to permitting the prosecution to conduct a cross-examination of the suspect without there being any opportunity for damaging admissions or misunderstandings to be set right by re-examination. And in many cases the end result would be that the suspect would agree to make a written and signed statement which in itself would justify a conviction without reference to the prolonged process of questioning which preceded it. The basic objective should be to eliminate interrogation of the kind developed in Northern Ireland from the criminal justice system.

One possible alternative would be to follow American practice and to provide that any statement taken from a suspect by the police should be inadmissible in evidence unless either it was taken in the presence of a legal adviser or the suspect had voluntarily waived his right to legal advice. This approach was given favourable consideration in the Fisher Report[41] and has been recommended to the Royal Commission on Criminal Procedure by the National Council on Civil Liberties.[42] One drawback to this approach in practice is that lawyers might well advise their clients not to submit to questioning or to make a statement. This difficulty was dismissed in the Fisher Report[43] on the ground that suspects could not properly be expected or required to say anything if

54

their lawyers advised against it. We are not convinced that this is a satisfactory answer, given the widely held view both in Britain and America that persons reasonably suspected of serious offences should be expected to submit to questioning, in the sense that the police should be able to put questions to them though not to require any reply. There would also be a serious risk that the police would continue their present practice of questioning suspects for long periods either under the pretence that they were voluntarily assisting them with their inquiries or by persuading them to waive their right to legal advice.

There is accordingly a strong case for the view originally put forward by Justice in 1967 that the questioning of persons reasonably suspected of serious offences should be conducted in a judicial setting before a magistrate or referee.[44] This approach would better meet the general view that it is perfectly right and proper to question such people provided that the questions are fairly put and without any improper pressure. It would also reduce the temptation for the police to continue to take suspects along to the station to 'help them with their inquiries'. We do not agree, however, that a procedure of this kind should be combined with a police power to arrest and hold suspects for questioning for a given number of hours, as in Northern Ireland under the Northern Ireland (Emergency Provisions) Act or as currently recommended by Justice.[45] What we are recommending is that the police would be empowered to question, before a magistrate, persons properly arrested on reasonable suspicion of an offence. In the case of the most serious offences the police already have a power to arrest on reasonable suspicion and to hold persons so arrested overnight. The definition of an arrestable offence is in our view much too wide for this purpose. But we think it reasonable that the police should have a power to arrest and hold suspects for a more restricted list of serious offences until they could be brought before a magistrate to submit to relevant questioning. Suspects might be granted an option of submitting to such questioning in the presence of their legal advisers where that would result in the matter being resolved more quickly, and should be entitled to legal aid or the services of a duty solicitor for the purpose. But the power to take the case before a magistrate would be necessary to secure co-operation of that kind. For less serious offences a power to require suspects to attend for questioning before a magistrate, or if they preferred their legal adviser, would be sufficient in itself and there would not be a need to arrest and hold for questioning. In respect of both categories of offence the ultimate obligation to bring any person arrested before a magistrate would act as a useful check on any tendency on the part of the police to engage in 'fishing expeditions' against 'known criminals' or to hold people for long periods to 'help them with their inquiries'.

Neither of these suggestions would interfere with the general right to silence, in the sense that no one would be required to give an answer to any question and in that the prosecution would still be required to prove their case beyond reasonable doubt in all cases including those in which the suspect had refused to say anything. But the failure of a suspect to say anything would clearly be a factor in the minds of a jury in making up its mind on guilt or innocence, just as the failure of a defendant to go into the witness box is now such a factor. No change in the right of the judge to comment on such matters would be involved, since it is already established law that the judge may draw the jury's attention to the failure of the defendant to give an explanation on relevant matters. The supposedly fundamental right to silence in this wider sense is and always has been largely illusory.

All this would clearly involve a major change in the role of magistrates in pre-trial proceedings. For the reasons which we shall give in the next chapter we are satisfied that such a change is long overdue.

6. THE COURTS

Special procedures for the trial of those charged with terrorist offences were recommended by the Diplock Commission in 1972 and introduced at the end of 1973. The Commission referred to three specific problems which had been encountered in securing convictions under ordinary criminal procedures.[1] In the first place the strict application of the common law rules on the admissibility of confessions had resulted in a substantial number of cases based on confessions obtained during prolonged interrogation being lost or withdrawn (see Chapter 5). In the second place there was concern about the possible intimidation of witnesses and jurors: in one well-publicised case in 1972 an important witness in a forthcoming case against an IRA suspect was shot dead shortly before the trial was due to begin. There was also concern about possible bias on the part of jurors. The pattern of jury selection and the practice of the prosecution to 'stand by' most Catholic jurors on the ground that they were specially open to bias or intimidation meant that in practice most juries were exclusively or predominantly Protestant, and there had been a number of allegedly perverse acquittals in cases against Loyalists.

The package of measures recommended by the Diplock Commission was specifically designed to overcome these problems. The extension of the powers of the police to arrest and question suspects, described in Chapters 4 and 5, was intended to facilitate the police in obtaining confessions from guilty suspects, and so to avoid any difficulty in securing convictions based on evidence from independent witnesses. Some change in the rules on admissibility was then thought to be necessary to avoid the risk that such confessions would be excluded by the judges: hence the provision that statements might be admitted provided that they had not been obtained by torture or inhuman or degrading treatment, also analysed in Chapter 5. Finally to avoid the risk of partisan or perverse verdicts trial by jury was suspended for a list of offences likely to be committed by terrorist offenders. These offences are known as 'scheduled offences' and the courts in which such cases are heard are generally referred to as 'Diplock Courts'.

There has been little effective change in the jurisdiction and operation of Diplock courts since their introduction. The initial list of scheduled offences covered murder and manslaughter, serious offences against the person, arson, malicious damage, riot, offences under the Firearms Act (Northern Ireland) 1969 and the Explosive Substances Act 1883, armed robbery and burglary, intimidation, membership of unlawful organisations and collecting information likely to be of use to terrorists, with a proviso that the Attorney General might certify that particular cases of murder, manslaughter and offences against the person should not be treated as scheduled offences.[2] Some minor changes in jurisdiction were made in 1975: the list of scheduled offences was extended to cover certain offences under the Prison Act (Northern Ireland) 1953, and the Prevention of Terrorism Act 1974 and offences committed in the Republic but tried in Northern Ireland under the Criminal Jurisdiction Act 1975.[3] Further provision was made for the effective descheduling of any scheduled offence tried summarily, in that the special rules on the admissibility of statements and on the burden of proof in respect of possession cases were removed for the purpose of summary trials. The ultimate decision on whether a scheduled offence shall be dealt with before a Diplock court nonetheless remains a matter for the prosecution, in that the defence has no means of challenging a decision either to refuse to deschedule a particular offence or to refuse to permit a summary trial in appropriate cases.

Trials in Diplock courts have in practice settled down to a regular legal routine. All cases on indictment are heard in Belfast where up to four or five Diplock courts are normally in session in the Crumlin Road courthouse. To the casual observer the proceedings would be more or less indistinguishable from those in an ordinary criminal trial.[4] The defendants sit in the dock surrounded by prison warders. There is a full complement of lawyers on either side, and the usual procession of witnesses who are examined and cross-examined in the usual way. The most obvious difference from an ordinary trial is the absence of a jury. But that in itself has a limited immediate impact in the majority of cases. In the first place there is a very high proportion of guilty pleas for which a jury would not in any event be empannelled. And in contested cases the major issue is frequently the admissibility of an alleged confession. In such cases the jury would be excluded from the hearing of evidence and legal argument on the issue of admissibility until the judge had ruled that the statement was admissible.

The overall nature of the evidence in most Diplock trials does have a significant impact on the nature of the proceedings. As has already been explained in Chapter 5, the basis of the prosecution case in the vast majority of cases is either a formal written statement by the defendant or an oral admission during questioning. There are rarely any witnesses whose evidence relates directly to the guilt or innocence of the defendant. Most are called only to establish that the particular shooting or bombing or other incident actually took place. Such witnesses, whether civilian or members of the security forces, are merely taken through their written depositions in a routine manner. The statement or admission by the defendant will then be produced. If the case is not contested the judge will convict and proceed directly to a consideration of any submission or evidence in mitigation before giving sentence. Such cases rarely last more than a few hours, unless there is a large number of charges or defendants. In contested cases the main issue is likely to be the admissibility and validity of the alleged confession or admission. The hearing of the evidence from all involved in the process of arrest and interrogation in what are termed 'statement fights' of this kind may take up to several weeks. But the focus of the proceedings is not on the alleged offences but on what happened in the police station. Much of the time is likely to be spent going over the various papers, documents and medical records concerning the defendant's time in police custody and the trial may well develop into a discussion between the judge and the lawyers of procedures and technicalities which lay observers, or a jury if there were one, would have some difficulty in following.

The Results of Diplock Trials

It is notoriously difficult to give a simple account of the results in any trial system. At each stage in the process there are a number of possible outcomes. The defendant may make an admission when he is first questioned. He may plead guilty to some or all of the charges against him, either initially or during the course of the trial. Some charges may be withdrawn by the prosecution either on formal legal grounds or in pursuance of what is generally known as a 'plea bargain'; that means that the defendant agrees to plead guilty to some of the other charges against him in exchange for an assurance that he will be treated leniently. He may contest the case and be acquitted by direction of the judge or by a decision of the jury on some or all of the charges against him. In addition there are frequently several defendants in each trial, some of whom are the principal offenders and some whose involvement is more peripheral. The outcome and sentence in respect of each defendant may differ appreciably. In Northern Ireland the picture is further complicated by the fact that some defendants refuse to recognise the legitimacy of the court in which they are being tried, and, therefore, refuse to enter any plea or to take any part in the proceedings. In such cases a plea of not guilty is formally entered on behalf of the defendant. But since no defence is offered, a refusal to recognise the court amounts for practical purposes to a plea of guilty, though the prosecution must, of course, bring some convincing evidence of guilt.

It is hardly surprising in view of this inherent and cumulative complexity that it is almost impossible to present a simple statistical analysis of trial outcomes which does not obscure or ignore important elements in the trial process. The nature of the problem may perhaps be illustrated by reference to the simple figures for the outcomes of Diplock trials from their introduction in 1973 until the end of 1979, set out in Table 6.1. These figures suggest that there has been a progressive increase in the proportion of guilty pleas and a substantial decline in the acquittal rate in contested cases. One possible explanation of this trend is that in the absence of juries, judges have become case-hardened and thus more ready to convict, and that defendants and their legal advisers have responded by pleading guilty in greater numbers in the hope of receiving a more lenient sentence. Another possibility, which has been much canvassed in official circles, is that the apparent decline in the acquittal rate is due to greater care on the part of the prosecuting authorities in the selection and preparation of cases.

Table 6.1: The outcomes of cases dealt with in Diplock courts from 1973 until 1979

Year	No. of persons	Pleaded guilty		Pleaded not guilty and found guilty		Acquitted		Apparent rate of acquittal in contested cases
1973	137	77	56%	37	27%	23	17%	38%
1974	1,228	723	59%	350	29%	155	13%	30%
1975	1,177	768	65%	323	27%	86	7%	21%
1976	991	668	67%	255	26%	68	7%	21%
1977	1,157	729	63%	371	32%	57	5%	13%
1978	910	673	74%	189	21%	48	5%	20%
1979	851	676	79%	137	16%	38	4%	22%

Notes: These figures refer to individual defendants in separate trials; a number of defendants appeared in several separate trials. Pleas of guilty refer to any plea of guilty on any one charge, not necessarily on all charges. Acquittals refer to those acquitted on all charges.

A more detailed consideration of the figures suggests that these are not the only explanations for the apparent trends shown in Table 6.1. The proportion of guilty pleas has been affected by the decline in the proportion of defendants refusing to recognise the court. If these defendants are treated as having effectively pleaded guilty the overall proportion of guilty pleas in earlier years increases, and in addition the acquittal rate in effectively contested cases is correspondingly increased. The effect of this adjustment for the periods covered by our more detailed sample surveys of outcomes is shown in Table 6.2.

This adjustment makes a substantial difference to the effective acquittal rate in contested cases, which rises to just over one third in the most recent years covered. The overall acquittal rate in effectively contested Diplock cases covered in Table 6.2 is 40%. This is not appreciably different from that reported in recent years in England and

Table 6.2: The effect of refusals to recognise the court on effective pleas of guilt and effective acquittal rates in contested cases for selected samples of cases

Sample year	No. of cases	Pleaded guilty	Found guilty Refused to recognise the court	Pleaded not guilty	Acquitted	Acquittal rate in contested cases Apparent	Effective
1973	150	89 59%	20 13%	17 11%	23 15%	38%	57%
1974	237	142 60%	25 11%	36 15%	32 13%	34%	47%
1975	467	249 53%	111 24%	65 14%	37 8%	17%	36%
1976	525	327 62%	80 15%	71 14%	39 7%	21%	35%
1979	359	264 73%	15 4%	47 13%	25 7%	29%	35%

Notes: A small number of cases not proceeded with have been omitted from this table. In addition, a small number of defendants who refused to recognise the court were acquitted; these have not been included in the figures for refusals to recognise, but are included as acquittals.

Wales in respect of contested jury trials. In 1978 the overall figure for England and Wales was 47%.[5] But the adjustment does not affect the substantial decline in the acquittal rate in Diplock courts from about 50% in 1973 and 1974 to about 35% for 1975, 1976 and 1979. Whether this decline is due primarily to judges becoming case-hardened or, as the authorities argue, to greater care by the prosecuting authorities in the selection and preparation of cases cannot be conclusively established. But some light may be thrown on the issue by comparing the trends in acquittal rates in jury trials in Northern Ireland with those in Diplock trials.

The figures in Table 6.3 for all jury trials in Northern Ireland from 1974 to 1979 show that, as in Diplock trials, there has been a substantial increase in the proportion of guilty pleas and a slight decline in the crude acquittal rate. The proportion of guilty pleas was a good deal higher than that in Diplock trials. This may be due to a lower level of cases in which charges are brought on disputable evidence or, perhaps, to a higher general level of acceptance of the system of jury trials. Whatever the explanation the combination of an increasing proportion of guilty pleas and a slight decline in the proportion of acquittals resulted in a substantial increase in the effective acquittal rate in contested cases from a figure of four or five in ten in 1974 to 1976 to six in ten in 1977 to 1979. This was appreciably greater than the equivalent figures both for jury trials in England and Wales and for Diplock trials in Northern Ireland.

This increase in the acquittal rate in jury trials is of some significance in assessing the possible explanations for the decline in the acquittal rate in Diplock trials. The Director of Public Prosecutions is responsible for preparing cases for both types of trial, and it is reasonable to assume that similar care is taken and similar standards are applied in all cases. It follows that it is reasonable to eliminate differences in prosecution

61

practice as an explanation for the declining acquittal rate in Diplock trials. If it is further assumed that the proportion of innocent persons prosecuted during the period and the factors which influence the defendant in pleading guilty have remained reasonably constant, the contrasting trends in Tables 6.2 and 6.3 provide strong support for the view that the declining acquittal rate in Diplock trials is the result of judges becoming case-hardened. This conclusion, when combined with the fact that a very high proportion of cases in Diplock trials are wholly dependent on confessions obtained during interrogation, can only increase the general concern that the risk of innocent persons being convicted in Diplock courts is substantially greater than in jury trials.

Table 6.3: The outcome of jury trials in Northern Ireland from 1974 until 1979

Year	No. of persons tried	Pleaded guilty		Pleaded not guilty and found guilty		Acquitted		Acquittal rate in contested cases
1974	719	577	80%	88	12%	54	8%	38%
1975	650	532	82%	59	9%	59	9%	50%
1976	608	549	92%	27	4%	32	5%	54%
1977	720	638	89%	32	4%	50	7%	61%
1978	882	772	88%	49	5%	61	7%	59%
1979	994	891	90%	42	4%	61	6%	59%

Note: the base for this table is as for Table 6.1.

It will be clear even from this brief analysis how difficult it is to draw compelling conclusions from statistics on trial outcomes. The essence of the problem is that there is no ideal acquittal rate. A high figure may indicate either that large numbers of guilty defendants are being acquitted or that large numbers of innocent persons are being brought to trial. A low figure may equally mean that some innocent defendants are being convicted or that the prosecuting authorities are being unduly cautious in bringing apparently guilty suspects to trial. The essential point is that the outcome of any trial system should be seen as the culmination of a large number of prior decisions, each of which – the decision by the authorities on whether to prefer charges, the decision on which charges to prefer, the decision by the defendant to plead guilty or not guilty to some or all of these charges – is as significant as the final decision by the judge or jury in a contested case. In the discussion which follows more emphasis will be placed on the nature and quality of the decisions which are being made at the various stages in the trial process in Diplock courts and on the relationship between them than on particular rates and proportions.

Diplock Trials in 1979

The cases on which this discussion is based are those tried in Diplock courts between January and April 1979. This is the same sample of cases as was discussed in Chapter 5. But since a number of individuals appeared in several separate trials before different judges the total number of cases is somewhat higher. In carrying out the analysis we have attempted to group together the cases in which similar important decisions were made by the prosecution or the defence at particular stages in the trial process. In the first place there were a few cases in which the prosecution decided not to pursue the case. Then there was a very large group of cases in which the defence decided not to contest the charges. In most of these a plea of guilty was entered. But in a few the defendant refused to recognise the court. In the remaining cases there was some element of contest. In some the defence and prosecution entered into a kind of bargain as a result of which some charges were withdrawn by the prosecution in exchange for a plea of guilty to the remaining charges. In others some or all of the charges were contested by the defence, with or without success. The numbers involved in each group are set out in Table 6.4. Since the strategy pursued by different categories of defendants and their lawyers differed substantially the sample has been further subdivided into three groups: Loyalist defendants, Republican defendants and members of the security forces charged with scheduled offences in the course of their duties. For example, there was a noticeable tendency for a higher proportion of Loyalists than Republicans to plead guilty and only Republicans refused to recognise the court. In addition a much higher proportion of Loyalists engaged in plea bargaining. But among the 'contesters' only Republicans were successful in obtaining complete acquittals. The pattern in cases against members of the security forces on the other hand, was completely different with one plea of guilty and a very high acquittal rate.

The Selection of Charges

The first stage in the trial process is the selection of charges. The initial decision on whether to initiate proceedings is entirely in the hands of the police. As we have explained in Chapter 5, this decision is effectively made after arrest and interrogation in that about two-thirds of those arrested and interrogated are not charged and in that the vast majority of charges are based upon a confession or admission obtained during interrogation. The choice of initial charges is also a matter for the police. Generally speaking there is a tendency for the police to select the most serious available charges in respect of each incident. Thus where an attack has been made on the security forces it is usual for the police to prefer a charge of murder or attempted murder, or at least a charge of shooting with intent to endanger life under section 14 of the Firearms Act (Northern Ireland) 1969. There is some justification for this policy in purely legal terms, in that it is technically easier to reduce

Table 6.4: The outcomes of trials in Diplock courts between January and April 1979

	Not proceeded with		Co-operators		Partial co-operators		Contesters		Not guilty plea to all			Total
	No appear-ance	Nolle prosequi	Plea of guilty to all	Plea of guilty to some, rest with-drawn	Plea of guilty to some, found guilty of others	Plea of guilty to some, not guilty of others	Refused to rec-ognise court, found guilty of all	Found guilty of all	Found guilty of some	Acquitted of all		
Loyalists	–	–	57 56%	33 32%	3 3%	–	–	7 7%	2 2%	–	102	100%
Republicans	2 1%	6 2%	123 50%	38 15%	2 1%	5 2%	15 6%	27 11%	10 4%	18 7%	246	100%
Members of security forces	–	–	1 12%	–	–	–	–	–	–	7 87%	8	100%
Total*	2 1%	6 2%	183 51%	71 20%	5 1%	5 1%	15 4%	34 10%	13 3%	25 7%	359	100%

*includes three cases in which defendant could not be identified as Loyalist or Republican.

charges than to increase them. But there is probably also a desire on the part of the police to prefer serious charges, particularly of murder, in order to be in a position to make public statements that a certain number of persons have been arrested and charged each week or month. There is strong political pressure on the police to produce results of this kind, particularly in the period from 1976 to 1979.

The most noticeable difference in the selection of charges against Loyalist and Republican defendants in our sample was in respect of membership of proscribed organisations.[6] Republicans were charged with this offence as a sole or principal charge in 28 cases, compared with a single Loyalist. Similarly in 42% of the cases against Republicans a membership charge was included along with other more serious charges, compared with only 10% of the cases against Loyalists. This difference was probably due in part to the differences in organisation and recruitment on the Loyalist and Republican sides. But there were at least 10 cases in our sample in which there was some reference in the court file to the defendant's connection with the UVF but no formal charge of membership. There must accordingly be some suspicion that the police make use of membership charges as a means of asserting control over young Republicans, but do not do so in the case of young

Table 6.5: Decisions on remand and bail applications in respect of persons tried in Diplock courts from January to April 1979

	Remanded in custody		Bail application granted		Other	
Loyalists	63	62%	30	29%	9	9%
Republicans	165	69%	66	27%	10	4%
Total*	230	66%	96	27%	20	6%

*including three cases not identified as Loyalist or Republican.

Loyalists. Many of the young Republicans dealt with in this way spent considerable periods in custody, though half were granted bail and most, as will be seen, were given non-custodial sentences. This difference in the use of membership charges, when combined with the fact that more Republican than Loyalist organisations are proscribed, must raise doubts about this aspect of current emergency legislation.

Remand in Custody or on Bail

When the suspect has been formally charged he must then be brought before a magistrate. In ordinary criminal cases the magistrate is entitled either to remand the defendant in custody or to grant bail or even to dismiss the case forthwith. In practice there is no real consideration either of the evidence against the accused or of the choice of charges at this stage. It is sufficient for the police to inform the magistrate that they have evidence suggesting that the accused is guilty of an offence and that they require further time to prepare their case. This is reflected in the description of the initial charge as a 'holding charge'. The important issue is whether the accused is to be remanded in custody or on bail.

In the case of scheduled offences the initial judicial hearing is even less significant in that the power of magistrates to grant bail has been withdrawn. Bail may only be granted by a High Court judge, and a separate application must be made for this purpose.[7] The only practical function of the initial hearing is to ensure that the defendant knows of and exercises his right to legal aid. If the defendant has not already chosen a solicitor, he is likely to be referred to one or other of the large firms which specialise in defending Diplock cases for Loyalists and Republicans respectively. It is fair to say that the only Diplock defendants who are not legally represented at state expense are those who make a deliberate decision not to accept legal aid, usually because they refuse to recognise the court.

An application to the High Court for bail is normally made on the initiative of the defendant's newly appointed defending solicitor, who will instruct a barrister to present his case to the court. There is a separate statutory provision for legal aid for this purpose.[8] Such applications are most likely to be granted in the case of relatively minor offences or of juveniles. Bail may also be granted in cases where the judge is persuaded that there has been unnecessary delay in proceeding with the case.

Between August 1973 and December 1979 there were 8183 applications for bail in scheduled cases, of which 3101 were granted, a proportion of 37%. In the cases in our sample where bail was sought it was granted in just under one-third of the cases, as shown in Table 6.5. But it must be remembered that many defendants facing serious charges do not apply for bail on well founded advice that it would not be granted. There was no significant difference in the treatment of Loyalist and Republican defendants in this respect. In both groups the large majority of persons released on bail were peripheral offenders.

It does not follow from this apparently even-handed treatment of bail applications that there is no case for a change in the law or practice on bail. It seems likely that the requirement to make a separate application to the High Court for bail has resulted in rather fewer defendants being remanded on bail. There is concern in some quarters that some offenders have been held in custody for long periods for relatively minor offences, notably alleged membership of Fianna Eireann by juveniles. In the cases in our survey 42 defendants who were given non-custodial sentences had been refused bail, and a further 38 had been granted bail only after a substantial period in custody. The initial reason for imposing restrictions on the granting of bail by magistrates in respect of scheduled offences was to ensure equality of treatment for all offenders and to prevent the risk of serious offenders absconding while on bail. Since such a large proportion of defendants on scheduled charges are already obtaining bail in High Court applications and since allegations of discrimination, as opposed to unduly cautious decisions, are no longer a matter for concern, there is a strong case for the restoration of the right of magistrates to grant bail for scheduled as for other offences. A return to the ordinary rules of criminal procedure in this respect would also save a good deal of judicial time and public expense.

The Director of Public Prosecutions

The next important step in the proceedings is the consideration of the case by the Director of Public Prosecutions. The office of Director of Public Prosecutions for Northern Ireland was established in 1972 as part of the initial package of reforms imposed on the Northern Ireland government by Westminster and was intended to ensure the elimination of any bias in police prosecutions and thus to increase public confidence in the judicial system.[9] The Director is formally responsible, subject only to directions by the Attorney General, for the conduct of the prosecution in all serious cases. Paradoxically neither the Director himself nor his legal officers exercise any direct control over the decision by the police to prefer charges in the first place nor over the selection of those charges. That decision is made by a police legal department which has been set up specially to supervise the selection of charges and the preparation of prosecution files. In practice the Director can take no action of any kind until the police have submitted their file, outlining the charges which have already been preferred and the nature of the evidence on which they are based. This may take up to 16 weeks on average from the defendant's first appearance before a magistrate.

When the prosecution file eventually arrives at the Director's office the selection of charges to be pursued is carefully reviewed in the light of the evidence which the police have assembled. A number of additional or alternative charges may be added to ensure that the full range of possibilities in respect of each incident may be considered by the court. It is usual, for instance, for defendants found in personal possession of loaded firearms to be charged both with possession with intent to endanger life under section 14 of the Firearms Act and with possession in suspicious circumstances under section 19A. The police may also be instructed to obtain more evidence on particular points. In most cases, however, the police decision on the choice of major charges is confirmed. In the period from 1973 to 1979 the holding charge preferred by the police was withdrawn by the Director in only 564 out of 7,279 cases. But in some of these cases the change is significant. In 120 of the 683 cases in which the police had preferred charges of murder or attempted murder, those charges were withdrawn by the Director, though other less serious charges were frequently pursued. The most obvious explanation for this particular pattern of overcharging by the police in murder cases is the strong political pressure on them to produce results, which in crude terms means the production of press releases and statistics on the number of persons charged for murder and other serious crimes. In a few cases in which the prosecution depends entirely on a confession and in which complaints of ill-treatment during interrogation have been made the Director may take the view that the confession will not be admitted in evidence and withdraw all charges. In the period from 1977 to June 1980 15 cases were dropped on this ground. When the Director and his staff are satisfied that the proper charges have been selected and that all necessary evidence has been assembled, the case will then be brought forward for committal proceedings.

It seems clear from the evidence at our disposal that the Director has generally been able to exercise a valuable control over police prosecution practice and to ensure an even-handed approach in cases against Loyalists and Republicans. The major area for continuing concern over prosecution policy is in respect of charges against members of the security forces. In cases of this kind, particularly those arising out of disputed incidents in which civilians have been shot by soldiers or policemen, there is clearly a much higher likelihood of political interference. The current Attorney General, Sir Michael Havers, has admitted that such cases are discussed in detail with the Director.[10] The nature of the problem which these cases present will be discussed further below in the light of the outcome of the cases covered in our sample. For the moment it is sufficient to stress the limitations on the role of the Director. Both in respect of the initiation of charges by the police and in respect of possible directions from the Attorney General the Director is very far from being an entirely independent agent. He is able to carry out a quasi-judicial function at a particular stage in the prosecution process. But he is wholly dependent on the reports which are submitted to him by the police. As will become clear from our concluding discussion, a fully judicalised prosecution system would require much more substantial changes in both law and practice.

Committal Proceedings

Like the initial appearance before the magistrate, committal proceedings in respect of scheduled offences are more or less a formality. Almost every case is dealt with by the presentation of written depositions, known as a 'preliminary enquiry', rather than by the alternative and traditional procedure, known as a 'preliminary investigation', in which oral evidence is given by the prosecution witnesses to the magistrate. Under section 2 of the Northern Ireland (Emergency Provisions) (Amendment) Act 1975 the prosecution is entitled to ask that any scheduled offence be dealt with in this way, and a magistrate may only

68

hold an oral hearing if he considers that it is necessary in the inte
of justice. This provision has been interpreted in such a way ᴀꜱ ʟᴏ
restrict oral hearings to cases in which there is disputed evidence on
such matters as identification. It is a further indication of the desire
on the part of the authorities to streamline the judicial process by
eliminating any effective opportunity for the defence to put into
practice what is, in theory, an essential part of the adversarial system
of criminal justice, the right to challenge the prosecution case at the
committal stage.

In practical terms the function of committal proceedings for scheduled
offences is merely to give formal notice to the defendant and his legal
advisers of the charges and the evidence which they will have to face at
the trial. Neither the magistrate nor the defence is in a position to
exercise any effective control over the prosecution at this stage. The
magistrate has little option but to grant his formal approval to committal on the basis of the papers submitted to him. The defence is
limited to a consideration of whether there is any point in making an
initial or renewed application for bail. It would not be unreasonable to
claim that, from the point of view of the defendant, all the proceedings
to this point have been bureaucratic rather than judicial. What has been
happening in reality is that the various agencies of the state, the police,
the Director of Public Prosecutions and the court administration, have
been preparing the case for eventual trial without there being any
effective opportunity for the defendant or his lawyers to do anything
about it other than wait. This wait, as has been explained, may be for a
considerable period. The average time between initial arrest and committal in 1979 was about 26 weeks and the average time between
committal and trial a further 17 weeks. Thus defendants tried in 1979
had spent an average of some 43 weeks in custody or bail before having
any opportunity to put their side of the case. In our sample of cases
30% of defendants waited between six and 12 months and a further
20% waited more than a year. In 1980 the average period awaiting trial
has been much reduced due to the decline in the number of persons
being arrested and charged.

Defence Options

As the time for the trial approaches the power to influence the course
of events shifts from the prosecution to the defence. There are two
basic options for the defendant and his legal advisers: to co-operate
with the prosecution with a view to obtaining a more lenient sentence,
or to contest the case in the hope of securing an acquittal. Within this
framework, however, there is a wide range of different strategies which
may be pursued. Co-operation may range from a plea of guilty to all
charges to an attempt to persuade the prosecution to drop some charges
in return for a plea of guilty to others. Contesting the case may range

from the more or less symbolic contest in cases where the defendant refuses to recognise the court to a serious attempt to secure an acquittal on some or all charges. The most straightforward and frequently adopted positions on this continuum of co-operation will be discussed in turn. But underlying the whole process is the assumption by lawyers on both sides that there are tangible benefits to be obtained from co-operating in cases in which there is little or no chance of securing an absolute acquittal.

Pressure to Plead

The large majority of defendants in Diplock trials, as in almost every trial system, plead guilty. The overall figures in Table 6.1 show that the proportion of defendants pleading guilty to some or all charges had risen by 1979 to almost four in every five. The more detailed analysis in Table 6.4 shows that during the period of our survey 51% of defendants pleaded guilty to all charges and a further 23% to some charges.

The primary explanation of the high level of guilty pleas is the fact that the vast majority of defendants have already admitted their guilt in the police station. But it is also a fact that lawyers on both sides put strong pressure on defendants to co-operate in this way. The factual justification for the view that it pays to plead in terms of sentencing practice is discussed in greater detail below. But there are some more general considerations which influence the attitude of both prosecution and defence lawyers.

From the point of view of the prosecution it is obviously desirable to secure as many guilty pleas as possible, not least because it ensures the orderly and relatively speedy disposition of cases, an important bureaucratic concern in the administration of justice. The importance which the authorities attach to this was nicely illustrated during the period of our survey by a scheme for the initial arraignment of all Diplock defendants at the start of each monthly list of cases. The purpose of this new procedure was to find out which defendants were prepared to plead guilty and which were intending to contest the case against them, so that a list of trials could be prepared which would make the most efficient use of the judges' time and thus reduce the time spent awaiting trial by those who wished to plead guilty. To assist in this defence solicitors were asked to fill in a form indicating whether their clients intended to plead guilty and how long they thought the case would last. The defendants were then brought before the court on the first day of each monthly Commission, formally arraigned on the charges against them and asked to plead guilty or not guilty. Those who pleaded guilty would then be dealt with relatively quickly. The cases of those who pleaded not guilty would be put down for an extended trial at some later date. This in itself was an inducement to plead in that most defendants like to get their trial over as soon as possible. But the attempt to streamline the trial process in this way did not work. A substantial number of defendants were unwilling to plead guilty to all or any of the charges against them on their initial arraignment. Some of these defendants did in fact plead guilty when their case finally came up for trial, thus giving the appearance that they were changing their plea in the course of their trial. A more accurate description of what was happening was that defence lawyers were advising their clients to keep their options open until their cases were finally set down for trial. For the purposes of our tabulations we decided that it was best to ignore these apparent changes of plea and to record only the final plea entered at the trial proper. Court administrators likewise realised that the pleas entered on initial arraignment meant very little, and that the new procedure was not achieving its purpose of assisting in the orderly disposal of cases. It was abandoned in 1980.

It is more difficult to explain the extent to which defence lawyers co-operate by putting pressure on their clients to plead guilty. To the extent that a plea of guilty is likely to secure a lower sentence it is obviously in the interest of guilty defendants to plead, and this argument is undoubtedly put to defendants in the majority of cases. From a purely financial point of view it might be thought that there would be some advantage to defence lawyers in contesting more cases since lengthier proceedings would result in higher legal fees. This is probably true in the case of solicitors, who have only to prepare the case for trial. But the advantage to the barristers who have effective control over the conduct of the case would be minimal. In a relatively small and un-specialised Bar like that in Belfast the financial return to barristers from being available to act in other civil and criminal cases is such that long trials are not generally welcomed. There is in any event strong professional and institutional pressure on both solicitors and barristers to co-operate with officials in securing the orderly disposal of cases and to avoid the disapproval which judges are likely to express if their clients plead not guilty in cases in which there is no justifiable legal defence. In a system in which the same barristers are likely to be asked to handle prosecution and defence cases these pressures are well understood. The lawyers' twin duties to their clients in securing as low a sentence as possible and to the courts in securing the efficient processing of cases combine to reinforce the general attitude among defence lawyers that it is right and proper to put some pressure on their clients to plead guilty.

Plea and Charge Bargaining

There is a substantial criminological literature on the practice of plea bargaining, which is generally taken to refer to cases in which defence lawyers enter into negotiations with the prosecution with a view to securing the withdrawal of certain more serious charges or an assurance of a more lenient sentence in exchange for a plea of guilty.[11] The

71

advantage from the prosecutor's point of view is that the case can be disposed of more quickly with a consequent saving of time and cost. Plea bargaining in a more general sense might be taken to extend to cases in which the defendant is persuaded to plead guilty to all the charges against him in the expectation of a lower sentence.

It was not possible from our study of court files to obtain any direct evidence of negotiations between the defence and the prosecution or the judge over the sentence which was likely to be imposed if a plea of guilty was entered. But we have no doubt that such negotiation takes place in Diplock courts as in other British courts. In our discussions with those involved in the trial process we have also been referred to cases in which defence lawyers have been offered an opportunity to have a case dealt with by a particular judge thought likely to be lenient if a plea of guilty is entered, with the implicit threat that the defendant would have to take his chance with a less sympathetic judge if he contested the case. The fact that the scheme for early pleading on initial arraignment was thwarted by the refusal of many defence lawyers to declare their hand so far in advance of the trial is a further indication of the prevalence of plea or sentence bargaining of this kind.

There was more explicit evidence in the court files of what might more accurately be called 'charge bargaining', in which defence lawyers enter into negotiation with the prosecution with a view to securing the withdrawal of certain charges in exchange for a plea of guilty to other charges. This form of bargain was entered into quite regularly. The figures in Table 6.4 show that there were 71 cases, representing about 20% of all cases, in which the prosecution withdrew or substituted a number of charges which were already on the indictment sheet and in which the defence pleaded guilty to the remaining or substituted charges. In a number of cases, for instance, charges of murder were withdrawn in response to a plea of guilty to manslaughter; in others a charge of causing actual bodily harm was substituted for the more serious charge of wounding with intent; in others the serious charge of possessing a firearm with intent to endanger life, for which a maximum sentence of life imprisonment may be imposed, was withdrawn in response to a plea of guilty to the alternative and less serious charge of possession in suspicious circumstances.

The advantage to the defendant in charge bargaining is most obvious in respect of murder charges, since there is a mandatory life sentence for murder. A plea of guilty to manslaughter in such cases avoids the special stigma of a conviction for murder and restores the discretion of the judge in sentencing. In a number of cases in our sample those accused of involvement in murders clearly obtained a significant reduction in the effective sentence in this way. Equally substantial reductions in the effective sentence were undoubtedly obtained by charge bargaining in a number of cases in which young defendants had admitted to peripheral involvement in serious attacks on members of the security forces, for instance by acting as a scout. By pleading guilty to such relatively minor offences as obtaining information likely to be of use to terrorists these defendants avoided the risk involved in pleading guilty even as accomplices to the charges of murder, attempted murder and causing explosions with intent to endanger life which had been laid against them. For example, the prosecution agreed to withdraw charges of murder and possession of firearms against a defendant who had been only 15 years old at the time of the attack on an army patrol in 1973 and who had merely acted as a scout in return for a guilty plea to a charge of collecting information on army movements, for which he was given a suspended sentence of two years. In other cases the advantage was probably more marginal. In some the prosecution agreed only to withdraw charges in respect of one of a series of separate terrorist incidents for which similar sentences would probably have been imposed. In others the prosecution merely withdrew a less serious alternative charge when the defendant pleaded guilty to a more serious charge in respect of the same incident. In such cases the only advantage which the defendant is likely to gain is whatever reduction in sentence may be thought appropriate in return for a general plea of guilty.

It is difficult to establish conclusively that any specific reduction in sentence has been obtained by pleading guilty, whether as a result of an independent decision by the defence or after negotiation with the prosecution. But there is evidence from our sample of cases to suggest that lower sentences are generally imposed on those who co-operate by pleading guilty than on those who contest the case against them. The analysis in Table 6.6 shows a substantial difference in the type and length of sentence imposed on those who co-operated by pleading guilty to some or all of the charges against them and those who contested the case. Of those who co-operated 37% were given a non-custodial sentence compared with 9% of those who contested their case and none of those who refused even to recognise the court. There was a similar pattern in terms of the length of custodial sentence: more than three-quarters of the co-operators received a sentence of less than ten years compared with about one-third of the contesters.

It does not follow that these variations in sentence were a direct result of the defendant's decision to co-operate or contest. The type and length of sentence in any case depends on a large number of factors, notably the number and seriousness of the charges, the defendant's age and his previous record. Further analyses were therefore carried out in which these various factors were allowed for. Similar, though less striking, variations in sentence between co-operators and contestors were observed. It is hard to avoid the conclusion that defence lawyers are right to advise their clients that it pays to plead guilty unless there is a strong chance of acquittal.

Table 6.6: The nature and length of sentence imposed on those defendants who co-operated and those who contested the case against them in Diplock trials from January to April 1979

Type of sentence	Co-operators		Refused to recognise		Contesters	
Non-custodial	93	37%	–	–	4	9%
Custodial	160	63%	15	100%	43	91%
Length of custodial sentences						
1-3 years	54	33%	1	7%	7	16%
4-9 years	66	41%	3	20%	13	30%
10-20 years	26	16%	7	46%	16	37%
Life	14	9%	4	27%	7	16%
Total	253	100%	15	100%	47	100%

Note: Co-operators include defendants pleading guilty to all and defendants pleading guilty to some with rest withdrawn; contesters include defendants pleading not guilty to all and found guilty on some or all.

Similar results have been obtained from studies in Britain. Baldwin and McConville, for instance, analysed the sentences imposed on three groups of defendants in Birmingham: those who pleaded guilty well in advance of the trial, those who changed their plea to guilty just before or during the trial, and those who contested the case.[12] Though defendants in each group were matched in terms of sex, age, type and number of charges and previous record, it was found that of the three groups those who changed their plea at a late stage were less likely to receive a custodial sentence and, when they did, were likely to receive a shorter sentence than the other groups. This indicates that there may be an even greater advantage to the defendant from negotiating a plea of guilty than from making an initial plea of guilty.

Opinions vary on the extent to which it is appropriate for those who plead guilty to be treated more leniently than those who do not. The ready admission of guilt by a defendant is some indication of remorse or at least of a recognition that he has done something wrong. Some account might also perhaps be taken of the fact that those who co-operate are saving the time and expense of a contested trial. It is more difficult to justify granting the same or greater advantages to those who deliberately enter into negotiations on the matter. In such cases there is clearly a danger that the interests of justice will be subordinated to those of bureaucracy. There must also be some concern on the evidence of our sample of cases that the prosecution may be selecting charges in some cases with a view to strengthening their hand in the process of negotiation. Given that charges of murder or attempted murder are so rarely pressed in cases against peripheral defendants, particularly in the case of youngsters accused of assisting in serious attacks or incidents, there must be some suspicion that they are included mainly as a bargaining counter to assist the prosecution in obtaining a plea of guilt. This is an undesirable practice.

Contested Cases: Partial Pleas

There is a similarly wide range of possibilities within the general category of contested cases. The lowest level of contest is exemplified by cases in which the defendant pleads guilty to some but not all of the charges against him, without securing the co-operation of the prosecution in withdrawing the remaining charges. In our sample there were ten such cases, as shown in Table 6.4. In most of these the defendant was successful in the sense that the contested charges were either dropped or substituted by other less serious charges.

It seems likely that most of these cases involved an attempted charge bargain which was offered by the defence but rejected by the prosecution. But there were also cases in which the partial plea appears to have represented a more serious denial of guilt in respect of one of a number of separate incidents. There were four cases of this kind in our sample. In two of these the defendants were found guilty on all charges and in two they were effectively acquitted in that the contested charges were not pursued. Since the evidence on all these charges was essentially the same, an alleged confession by the defendant, and since the effective sentence was unlikely to be affected, these cases provide a further indication of the possible unreliability of confessions, particularly those obtained during prolonged interrogation.

Contested Cases: Refusing to Recognise the Court

The practice of refusing to recognise the court is also a form of partial contest. As will be clear from the figures in Table 6.2 the proportion of cases in which the legitimacy of Diplock courts has been formally challenged by defendants in this way has declined sharply. In the years from 1973 to 1976 this position was adopted mainly by committed Republicans on the general ground that they refused to recognise the legitimacy of any court in Northern Ireland since they refused to recognise the legitimacy of the state itself. A few Loyalists also refused to recognise the court in that period on the more specific ground that they objected to Diplock courts as such, and were thus in a sense asserting their right to jury trial. The sharp decline in the number of refusals to recognise by Republicans, and the absence of any on the part of Loyalists, appears to be due largely to the fact that defendants on both sides are now being instructed by their respective paramilitary organisations to recognise the court and to attempt to obtain either an acquittal or a less severe sentence in any case in which there is a real chance of doing so. Those who refused to recognise the court in our latest sample were for the most part experienced members of the IRA against whom there was ample independent evidence on a number of very serious charges and no realistic prospect of anything other than a very long sentence of imprisonment.

The increasing readiness of Republicans, and to a lesser extent Loyalists, to recognise the legitimacy of Diplock courts is in one sense surprising, given the sustained campaign on both sides against any form of special court and the associated claim for special category status for those convicted in them, which is discussed in greater detail in Chapter 7. The explanation appears to lie in the particular nature of the IRA and its counterparts. Those who take part in terrorist activities in Northern Ireland are not generally committed to any theoretical or intellectual position on the nature of state authority like that of such groups as the Bader-Meinhof terrorists in West Germany or the Red Brigades in Italy. As we have sought to show in Chapter 3, they are generally representative of the working class communities from which they are recruited and show the general deference of most members of that class to the lawyers and judges whom they meet in their passage through the courts.

Unsuccessfully Contested Cases

The largest group of contested cases in our sample were those in which the defendant pleaded not guilty to all the charges against him. In addition to the 15 cases of refusal to recognise the court there were 72 such cases, involving 55 Republicans, nine Loyalists and seven members of the security forces, as shown in Table 6.4. There was a substantial difference in the pattern of outcomes for these three groups of defendants. None of the Loyalists were acquitted. Of the Republicans 18 were completely acquitted, an acquittal rate of 33%. And all the members of the security forces were acquitted. It is difficult to justify such startling differences on the information available to us. A full assessment of the merits of the decisions could only be undertaken in the light of a detailed observation and analysis of what happened in each trial, which was not possible within the resources at our disposal. The comments which follow are based only on a study of the material in court files.

The most striking feature of the cases in which the defendant contested all charges but was convicted on all or most of them was the high proportion of alleged confessions. In at least three-quarters of the cases the defendants were alleged to have made a voluntary statement. In all but a few of these this was the only substantial evidence in the prosecution case, though there were a number of other cases in which there was also some indication that the defendant had been named by accomplices. The essence of the defence in many of these cases was clearly the inadmissibility of the alleged confession. In only about one-third of the cases for which full details of the initial prosecution cases were available to us did there appear to be strong independent evidence, by way of identification, fingerprints and the like, pointing to the guilt of the accused. Such heavy reliance on contested confessions, given the general doubts over the reliability of confessions obtained by prolonged interrogation discussed in Chapter 5, is itself a cause for concern and cannot but affect general public confidence in the standards of justice administered in Diplock trials.

Two examples of unsuccessfully contested cases involving both written and oral confessions may help to emphasise the point. In one case during the period of our survey a young man from Co. Tyrone was charged with murdering a policeman and with membership of the IRA. He alleged that a written confession had been obtained from him by physical ill-treatment and threats, and produced a witness in support of an alibi. There was some medical evidence in support of the allegations of ill-treatment, but it was not conclusive. The judge admitted the confession, rejected the alibi on the ground that the witness could not be sure of the date, and sentenced the defendant to life imprisonment.[13] In another case tried in December 1979 three men and a girl were charged with involvement in the murder of a policeman who had been identified from a photograph in a pigeon-fanciers magazine. Two of the men and the girl, who later changed her plea to guilty, made written statements admitting their involvement. The third man, who was alleged to have procured the murder as an IRA intelligence officer, refused to make any written statement, though he was interrogated for 49 hours over a period of four days; during the second day he was in the interrogation room for a continuous period of more than 11 hours. He denied making the oral admissions which the police claimed he had made on four separate occasions on the third and fourth days of interrogation. There was no other admissible evidence. The judge rejected the claim that the length and intensity of interrogation justified the rejection of the alleged oral admissions, and added that the defendant's refusal to make a written statement was evidence that he had not lost control of himself as a result of the prolonged interrogation. All three male defendants were sentenced to life imprisonment.[14]

Acquittals

There was a similar pattern in the 18 cases which were successfully contested by Republican defendants. In about half the cases the acquittals appear to have been the result of the rejection of alleged confessions. For the most part these alleged confessions appear to have been ruled inadmissible on the ground of physical ill-treatment during interrogation. But in one case a confession was ruled inadmissible on the ground that it had been obtained by trickery, that is by a promise to the defendant that if he confessed his statement would not be used in evidence.[15] In another an alleged confession by one defendant was apparently rejected because it was clearly inconsistent with another alleged confession by a co-defendant: one of the two alleged confessions described the hoax bomb placed on a bus as a shoebox with a brick in it while the other referred to a potato-crisp carton.

In the remaining cases there was no admission of guilt by the defendant and the defence was apparently able to persuade the judge that his story was at least as convincing as that of the prosecution witnesses. For instance in one case the identification of an allegedly wanted man by a soldier in an observation position close to the scene of a bombing was rejected in favour of an alibi by the defendant in spite of the fact that — or perhaps because of it — the soldier claimed that he was 'trained at identification'. In two other cases defendants persuaded the judge that they had been forced to keep firearms in their houses.

Perhaps the most surprising feature of this group of cases was the absence of any Loyalist acquittals. There was no obvious difference in the nature of the cases contested by Loyalists, nor any apparent difference in the range of defences raised. There were, for instance, a number of cases in which the defence claimed that alleged confessions had been obtained by ill-treatment during interrogation. It can only be surmised that the prosecution case against Loyalists was generally stronger, or perhaps that the generally greater willingness on the part of Loyalists to co-operate resulted in the withdrawal of doubtful cases at an earlier stage.

Nolle Prosequis

The possibility that weaker cases are sometimes pursued further against Republicans than against Loyalists is given some additional support by the fact that all the cases in which charges were withdrawn by the entry of *nolle prosequis* by the Director of Public Prosecutions or by findings of 'no bill' were against Republican defendants. There were six such cases in our sample. In four cases the defendants were almost certainly guilty of a technical offence, such as the failure to disclose information to the police. In two other cases the defendants had already been convicted of much more serious offences and there was clearly little point in pursuing the remaining relatively minor charges against them. We see no reason to criticise the prosecuting authorities for their decision not to pursue these cases. In the remaining two cases listed in Table 6.4 as 'not proceeded with' the defendants had been released on bail and did not turn up for their trials.

Cases Against Members of the Security Forces

A less surprising but equally worrying feature of the successfully contested cases was the 100% acquittal rate in cases against members of the security forces. Of the seven cases in our sample five were against police officers and two against soldiers. Three of the police officers were allegedly involved in serious assaults on a suspect under interrogation at Armagh. Two were allegedly involved in similar assaults on a suspect in Omagh. As we have already made clear in Chapter 5, these prosecutions represent only a tiny minority of the total number of cases in which serious complaints of assault during interrogation are made against the police. Though one of the two trials in our sample was the result of a private prosecution, the prosecution case as revealed in the court file of depositions was not inherently implausible, in that there were independent medical witnesses. The two cases against soldiers likewise involved allegations of assault in the course of an arrest or search by Army street patrols which both sides agreed developed into a brawl. In one of these cases the victim later died of injuries received from a rifle butt in the stomach. The remaining case against a soldier, in which the defendant pleaded guilty, involved a similar but much less serious incident during a vehicle search operation.

The fact that all the defendants in this group who contested the charges against them were acquitted can be explained only in terms of a different approach by the prosecuting authorities or the courts to such cases. The prosecuting authorities have on occasions indicated that the decision on whether to prosecute soldiers and policemen causes special difficulty in that the evidence almost always amounts to a straight conflict between the complainant and the policemen or soldiers concerned, who usually outnumber the complainant or complainants. It has been suggested that one reason for the high acquittal rate is that prosecutions are sometimes authorised in cases in which the evidence falls short of that which would be required for a normal prosecution to meet the public demand for some action to be taken over particular incidents. Our own view is that the pattern of outcomes in these cases is better explained by the fact that a higher standard of proof is effectively required to rebut the general presumption that policemen and soldiers are more trustworthy than those who make complaints against them. When the effect of this presumption is combined with the fact that no admissions are made by the defendants and that the very strong group loyalty of those serving in the police and the army usually secures a completely united front from all defendants and witnesses, the difficulty in securing convictions can be understood, if not justified. It should be noted that this problem is not confined to Diplock courts. Similar low conviction rates in jury trials of policemen have been a cause for concern in Britain and elsewhere. It is for this reason that we share the view of the Bennett Committee that the threat of criminal prosecution should not be regarded as the most effective means of controlling malpractice in the use of emergency powers.[16] There is nonetheless a strong case for the introduction of a stronger element of independent lay participation in the trial of these charges, if only to strengthen public confidence in the administration of this aspect of criminal justice.

A Return to Jury Trial?

There remains the more general issue of whether the continued suspension of jury trial for scheduled offences is justified in the light of the results in the sample of judge-only trials which we have analysed. The decision to dispense with juries in Diplock trials was based primarily on the fear that jurors might be intimidated. But there was also some evidence of perverse acquittals of Loyalists by predominantly Protestant juries. It is clear from our sample of cases that there was no question of any similar bias on the part of judges in cases against Loyalists. On the other hand, there is some evidence both from the declining acquittal rate in contested Diplock trials and from the somewhat higher rate of acquittal in jury trials in Northern Ireland and in Britain that judges may have become case-hardened and are thus no longer in a position to give to the defendant the full benefit of his right to acquittal in any case where the prosecution has not proved its case beyond reasonable doubt. There must also be some concern over the extent to which contested cases in Diplock courts are based predominantly or exclusively on alleged confessions which are later repudiated by the defendant.

Few people now claim that juries are inherently better than judges at assessing evidence or deciding difficult issues of fact.[17] The argument for retaining the right of jury trial is based on the more general ground that a panel of randomly selected citizens which has to deal only with a single case, or at a most limited number of cases, is free from the danger of case-hardening. It is also better able to take a commonsense rather than a legalistic view of weak prosecution cases and to bring in a not guilty verdict in cases in which, while the defendant may have been technically guilty, the police or the prosecution have acted in such a way as to make a conviction inappropriate. On the other hand there is probably a greater risk of prejudice or bias by jurors than by judges, and, in the special conditions prevailing in Northern Ireland, the possibility that individual jurors will be intimidated or feel themselves at risk if they take part in the conviction of members of paramilitary organisations cannot be ignored.

Despite these risks there is a strong case in our view for the reintroduction of some element of lay participation in the trial of scheduled offences. In the first place it would provide an important safeguard against case-hardening on the part of judges. It would in particular be of assistance to judges in resolving the very difficult decisions which have to be made in cases which involve contested confessions or charges against members of the security forces. It would also emphasise the public nature of the trial process and help to prevent it becoming the bureaucratic preserve of lawyers and officials. Finally it would permit members of the public in Northern Ireland to exercise the traditional role of the jury in controlling the abuse of state power.

There is equally a strong case for the adoption of the suggestion by the Standing Advisory Commission on Human Rights that the decision on the admissibility of contested confessions should be taken in a separate trial held as soon as possible after the alleged ill-treatment or breach of regulations.[18] This would not only permit an independent decision to be made on whether an alleged confession could be used at a subsequent trial. It would also provide an opportunity for an independent assessment of the merits of any complaints about the conduct of interrogations, and might form the basis of subsequent disciplinary or criminal proceedings against police officers found to have acted in breach of the code of practice which we have recommended. Some element of lay participation, whether by the appointment of special assessors or by empannelling a special jury, should be introduced in this process.

Whether lay participation in the final stage of Diplock trials should be achieved by an immediate return to ordinary jury trial is less certain. As in other aspects of emergency powers a gradual but deliberate return to normality is more likely to prove practicable. In the first place the list of scheduled offences should be reduced to ensure that the right to jury trial is suspended only for those cases in which there is a serious risk of intimidation. There were a number of cases in our sample, particularly minor cases of robbery by young offenders pretending to have guns, in which there was no evidence of any paramilitary connection. The definition of a scheduled offence should be revised to ensure that only those cases in which there is evidence that the offence was committed on behalf of a paramilitary organisation are covered. This would have the added advantage of ensuring that members of the security forces were tried before a jury, which we believe to be of special importance in securing public acceptance of the ultimate verdict. In addition the Director of Public Prosecutions should be authorised to deschedule offences other than those of murder or offences against the person in appropriate cases. To avoid the kind of bias in jury selection and challenge which ensured that Catholics would be excluded from most cases, as described in *Law and State*,[19] the law and practice of jury vetting and challenging should be reviewed.

In the remaining scheduled cases an element of lay participation could be achieved by the appointment of lay assessors. This practice is already established in juvenile courts in Northern Ireland. Its extension to the trial of scheduled offences would help to counteract the danger of case-hardening on the part of judges and to reduce the burden of decision-making in difficult contested cases. Given the very high proportion of uncontested cases the practical problems of providing lay assessors would not be unduly great.

Changes in the Rules of Evidence

Two further changes in the rules for the trial of scheduled offences are essential to secure greater public acceptance of the system. In the first place the provisions of section 8 of the Northern Ireland (Emergency Provisions) Act 1978 which permits the admission in evidence of statements obtained during interrogation provided that it is established that they have not been obtained by torture or inhuman or degrading treatment should be repealed. Despite the stand taken by judges on the interpretation of this section, its very existence and lack of precision provides an excuse for those involved in interrogation to ignore the ordinary rules of the common law and the Judges Rules. As we have already argued in Chapter 5, it should be clearly provided that statements obtained during interrogation are admissible evidence only if it is shown that the statutory code of practice for such interrogation which we have recommended has been adhered to.

Provision should also be made to ensure that convictions cannot be obtained purely on the basis of confessions which have been obtained during interrogation and subsequently challenged by the defence. For the reasons which we have explained in Chapter 5 such confessions are not always reliable, and should therefore require corroboration, just as identification evidence now requires some corroboration. The main purpose of the requirement of corroboration in both cases is to avoid the danger of unjust convictions. But in the case of confessions it would also help to discourage detectives from relying wholly on the process of interrogation and encourage them to engage in rather more traditional detective work. There were a number of cases in our sample in which the police appear to have been content to rely on confessions and thus not to follow up other lines of enquiry. Some continuing protection for civilian witnesses by way of anonymity is still necessary in the conditions prevailing in Northern Ireland. But the objective should be to involve members of the public in the administration of justice insofar as is practicable.

Sentencing

It is notoriously difficult to assess the consistency and fairness, let alone the efficacy, of sentencing. Numerous factors may influence the decision in each case: the number and seriousness of the charges, the extent of the defendant's involvement, his age, his previous criminal record and his employment prospects, and the extent to which he has co-operated with the prosecution or shown remorse for his crimes. Since 1974 more than 6,000 offenders have been sentenced in Diplock courts. Many of them have been given very long sentences of imprisonment. Many others have been given non-custodial sentences. It is thus very easy to produce startling comparisons in the treatment of two apparently similar cases, or in the treatment of Loyalist and Republican defendants for particular offences. There have been a number of well-publicised complaints of injustice of this kind.

In our analysis of the performance of Diplock courts in 1979 and in earlier years we have attempted to assess complaints of this kind, both on a general level and in respect of specific cases. We have not in recent years been able to establish any clear evidence of systematic discrimination, though we have come across individual cases in which there appears to have been undue leniency or severity. It is impractical to reproduce here all the tabulations and analyses which we have carried out on our latest sample, and on which we have based our conclusions. But some indication can be given of the nature and range of sentences imposed, of the differences in treatment of Loyalist and Republican offenders and of the reasons for those differences.

In the tabulations which follow we have adopted certain conventions to simplify the presentation. In the first place we have treated each defendant as having been given a single sentence, instead of a separate sentence for each charge for which he is convicted. For this purpose we have selected the offence for which the heaviest sentence was imposed. Where two offences were given the same sentence the offence for which the highest statutory maximum sentence is provided was selected and where the statutory maximum was the same the offence which reflected the nature of the incident. For example in cases in which charges of armed robbery and of unlawful possession of fire-arms were combined, we have classified the case as robbery.

The figures in Tables 6.7 and 6.8 show the nature of the sentence imposed on Loyalist and Republican offenders analysed in this way, and the length of sentence imposed in cases in which a custodial sentence was awarded. It is clear from this analysis that a much higher proportion of Republicans are given a non-custodial sentence, but that there is little variation in the average length of the custodial sentences imposed on Loyalists and Republicans.

Table 6.7: The sentence imposed on the most serious charge for which each defendant was found guilty

	Non-custodial		Custodial sentence on juveniles		Imprisonment		Total	
Loyalists	18	18%	5	5%	79	77%	102	100%
Republicans	82	37%	12	5%	126	57%	220	100%
Total*	100	30%	17	5%	208	65%	325	100%

includes three cases not identified as Loyalist or Republican.

There are a number of factors which may help to explain this pattern in respect of custodial and non-custodial sentences. The most important is that Loyalists were proportionately more likely to be found guilty of murder, attempted murder, manslaughter, and robbery, while Republicans were proportionately more likely to be found guilty of firearms and explosives offences and of such relatively minor offences as hijacking and membership of an illegal organisation. Non-custodial sentences were much more likely to be imposed in respect of this latter category: two-thirds of those convicted of such offences were given a non-custodial sentence. In respect of membership charges, in cases in which that was the most serious charge for our purposes, a non-custodial sentence was imposed on 25 out of 28 defendants.

Table 6.8: The length of custodial sentence imposed on the most serious charge for which each defendant was found guilty

	Custodial sentence on juveniles		1-3 years		4-6 years		7-9 years	
Loyalists	5	6%	17	21%	20	24%	11	13%
Republicans	12	9%	30	22%	29	21%	25	18%
Total*	17	7%	48	21%	50	22%	36	16%

	over 10 years		Life		Total	
Loyalists	15	18%	16	19%	84	100%
Republicans	33	24%	9	7%	138	100%
Total*	49	21%	25	11%	225	100%

*includes three cases not identified as Loyalist or Republican.

Within the main offence categories there was also some variation in respect of custodial and non-custodial sentences. For instance, only one out of 13 Loyalists whose principal offence was an offence against the person received a non-custodial sentence compared with six out of 25 Republicans; similarly only three out of 32 Loyalists compared with six out of 25 Republicans who were charged with robbery received a non-custodial sentence; but in respect of cases in which a firearms offence was the principal offence six out of 19 Loyalists compared with only 13 out of 47 Republicans received a non-custodial sentence. A closer examination of these individual cases suggests that this variation can be explained in relation to the seriousness of the incident, the extent of the offender's involvement or the strength of the evidence. For instance, of the six Republicans who were given a non-custodial sentence for robbery two were convicted of robbing a shop-keeper of £45 with a toy gun, one was convicted only of keeping watch while the robbery was carried out and the remaining three appeared to have played only a minor role in the commission of the offence. A similar pattern was observable in respect of firearms charges. For instance, in six of the cases against Republicans the charge was of possession of firearms only in the sense that the offender had admitted to having handled a gun at an arms training session. In another case in which a young offender was convicted of serious arms charges and awarded a suspended sentence of eight years it was clear that he had acted only as a scout.

The main reason for the greater proportion of non-custodial sentences in respect of Republican offenders in more general terms would appear to be that the net of criminal justice is cast more widely in respect of Republicans than in respect of Loyalists. This was most clearly observable in respect of membership charges, as we have already pointed out. But there was also some indication that Republicans were more likely than Loyalists to be charged with peripheral involvement in offences or with failure to co-operate with the security forces in giving information. This form of discrimination was to some extent compensated at the sentencing stage. But a number of those involved had already spent considerable periods in custody.

We have carried out a similar detailed analysis of the length of custodial sentences imposed on Loyalists and Republicans. In this respect, as the figures in Table 6.8 indicate, there was a much greater degree of similarity in the range of sentences imposed, and this was maintained when such factors as the nature and seriousness of the principal offence and the offenders' previous records were taken into account. Though there were a number of cases in which different sentences were imposed for apparently similar offences, we could find no evidence of any systematic variation. The most publicised recent case involved the suspended sentence imposed by the Lord Chief Justice early in 1980 on members of the RUC convicted of involvement

Table 6.9: The outcome of appeals from Diplock trials, 1977-79

Appeals against conviction	Total entered	Withdrawn	Dismissed	Upheld	Success rate
1977	39	6 (15%)	29	4	12%
1978	56	29 (52%)	23	4	14%
1979	82	65 (79%)	13	4	24%
Appeals against sentence					
1977	107	30 (28%)	54	23	31%
1978	102	55 (54%)	38	9	19%
1979	137	104 (76%)	25	8	24%

in the kidnapping of a Catholic priest; this was in sharp contrast with the long prison sentence imposed on a Republican defendant for a similar offence, and emphasises further the different standards which appear to be applied in cases involving members of the security forces.

Appeals

We have not been able to carry out any detailed analysis of the outcome of appeals in the cases in our sample, mainly as a result of the long delays in some cases and of the difficulty in obtaining full details of the court file in these cases. But some indication of the relative lack of significance of the appeal system is given by the figures on the outcome of all appeals entered and disposed of in the period from 1977 to 1979. It is clear from these figures that, while appeals were entered in a large proportion of cases, rising from 13% in 1977 to 26% in 1979, most were abandoned. Of those which were pursued there was a tendency, as might be expected, for appeals against sentence to be rather more successful than appeals against conviction.

Conclusions

It is fair to conclude on the basis of this analysis that the Diplock court system has continued to operate without discrimination and that from the point of view of the authorities it has worked smoothly and efficiently. But this bureaucratic success has been achieved at a high cost in terms of public acceptability and confidence in the system of criminal justice.

The elimination of discrimination has been achieved both by the assertion of independent control over the prosecution process and by the suspension of jury trial. The pattern of outcomes and sentencing in Diplock courts does not provide any evidence of systematic bias on the part of the judges against Republican defendants. On the contrary our figures on acquittals and on the proportion of non-custodial sentences suggests that Republicans fared rather better than Loyalists, though we believe that this was largely due to differences in prosecution policy at the police stage, in that charges of peripheral involvement and of membership of illegal organisations were more likely to be pursued against Republicans than Loyalists. On the other hand there is some indication that the suspension of jury trial has led to a slight decrease in the effective acquittal rate, and that this is due to case-hardening on the part of the judges. About one in three contested cases resulted in an acquittal, compared with a corresponding figure of between four and five in ten in jury trials both in Northern Ireland and in Britain. The suspension of jury trial may also be related to the very high acquittal rate in cases against members of the security forces. We have accordingly recommended the reintroduction of some element of lay participation in the decision on guilt, and the curtailment of the list of scheduled offences.

The efficient operation of the Diplock court system, however, is largely dependent on confessions which have been obtained during prolonged interrogation. A very large number of convictions are based entirely on such confessions, and a high proportion of contested cases revolve around their admissibility and reliability. Even if the vast majority of such confessions are true the fact that they have been obtained under oppressive circumstances and the risk that a few may be false has a serious impact on general public confidence in the judicial process. We have accordingly recommended two important changes in

the rules of evidence: that confessions should be admissible in eviden
only where it is shown that a statutory code of interrogation practice
has been complied with, and that some corroboration should be required
in all cases in which a confession has been obtained during interrogation.

These recommendations are all made on the assumption that the
system of Diplock courts is retained only on a temporary basis and that
there will be a gradual and deliberate return to reliance on normal
criminal procedures. Even if the temporary emergency procedures
were ended immediately, however, this would not affect the equally
significant longer term trend towards the bureaucratisation of the trial
process and shifting of the effective decision on guilt or innocence from
the court room to the police station. This trend, and the associated
pressure on defendants to plead guilty, is not restricted to Northern
Ireland. Judicial controls over the pre-trial stages in the criminal process
have been progressively eroded throughout the common law world.
There is a strong case for the reassertion of judicial as opposed to
bureaucratic values in the whole criminal process and for the reactivation
of effective judicial supervision at the pre-trial stages in that process. We
have already argued in Chapter 5 that provision should be made for
judicial involvement in the process of questioning. Similar provisions
are required to ensure the proper supervision of the collection of
evidence, the selection of charges and the process of plea bargaining.

As in the case of judicial involvement in the questioning process,
most of the necessary changes could be made by reactivating the
functions of magistrates at the pre-trial stages. As part of their function
of reviewing the evidence submitted by the prosecution at the committal stage we believe that magistrates should be encouraged and if
necessary enabled to require the prosecution to produce relevant
evidence or relevant witnesses. Magistrates and judges should also be
prepared to exert more control over the selection of charges and the
withdrawal of charges in exchange for pleas of guilt. It should also be
made much clearer that while some diminution of sentence may be
expected for those who are prepared to admit their guilt and give some
indication that they accept that they have done wrong, no additional
advantage can be obtained by entering into negotiation on these matters.

None of these suggestions are intended to lead towards an inquisitorial
system of trial. The primary function of investigation would remain
with the police, and the primary function of preparing the prosecution
case would remain with the Director of Public Prosecutions. What is
involved is some limitation on the freedom of the police and the
prosecutor to make what decisions they please and to enter into whatever bargains with the defence will help to secure their bureaucratic
objectives. We do not believe that there can be any serious objection to
some interference with the pure adversarial model of criminal procedure
in the general interests of justice.

7. THE PRISONS

The prison system in Northern Ireland has been under severe strain since the introduction of internment in 1971. The total number of prisoners in custody increased from a daily average of about 600 in 1968 and 1969 to more than 2,650 by 1974.[1] By 1980 the figure had declined only slightly to some 2,500. In the early period there were continuing complaints about conditions, particularly in the hutted compounds in the Long Kesh internment camp outside Belfast. This culminated in a serious riot on 15 October 1974 during which many of the huts were burned down. There were 'sympathy' disturbances at Magilligan and Armagh prisons. Since then most of the compound accommodation at Long Kesh, which was renamed Maze Prison in 1972, and Magilligan has been replaced by permanent cellular accommodation, popularly known as 'H Blocks' because of their design. By 1980 the number of prisoners in hutted compounds had been reduced to about 500.

Special Category Status

Throughout this period the question of the status of various categories of prisoners has perhaps been of even greater significance than their physical conditions. Like many other issues in Northern Ireland the problem is a mixture of historical development and of incompatible principles. When internment was introduced on a large scale in 1971 those who were detained were not treated like ordinary convicted criminals. They were housed in hutted compounds at Long Kesh and Magilligan and permitted to organise themselves within those compounds rather like prisoners of war. They were also granted the same rights and privileges regarding visits, letters and parcels, and wearing their own clothes like unconvicted prisoners on remand.

In June 1972 similar privileges were granted to members of para-military organisations who had been convicted in the courts for terrorist activities, but who claimed to have been politically motivated and were accepted by compound commanders. This concession of 'special category status' was made partly in response to a hunger strike by some convicted Republican prisoners and partly to facilitate the negotiations which were then under way between the British government and the Provisional IRA. The special treatment of convicted paramilitary offenders was thus introduced before the establishment of Diplock courts. But it was natural to extend the concession to all those who were convicted of scheduled offences in Diplock courts after 1973.

The system of detention in compounds, both for those who had been interned without trial and for those who had been convicted but granted special category status, worked reasonably well. In practice each compound was allocated to a particular paramilitary group, so that neither Loyalists and Republicans nor members of the Official and Provisional IRAs were expected to live with each other. Inside each compound there was a commanding officer who organised the daily routine of washing, cleaning and eating and whatever political or military education was thought appropriate. Direct contact with prison staff was minimal. Warders did not enter the compounds except for regular morning and evening headcounts, for which inmates might be expected to parade, and occasional search operations which were carried out to prevent the accumulation of weapons and other prohibited articles within the compounds. Food was passed through the control gate at the entrance to each compound. But its distribution was a matter for the inmates. Inmates required for visits or other official purposes were called for from the control gate and would then be escorted by warders to other parts of the prison.

This system clearly afforded a great deal of autonomy to paramilitary groups within the prison system and was in effect a recognition by the authorities of a form of political status for terrorist offenders. It was strongly criticised by the Gardiner Committee in 1975 on a number of grounds: that special category prisoners were more likely to emerge with an increased commitment to terrorism; that it led them to regard themselves as detainees rather than convicted prisoners, and to expect an eventual amnesty; and that its legality under the Prison Rules was doubtful.[2] As part of its long term strategy of phasing out internment and relying on convictions in Diplock courts the Committee recommended that the earliest practicable opportunity should be taken to end special category status, and that it should be made absolutely clear that there would be no amnesty for special category prisoners.

This recommendation was eventually put into effect. As internment was being phased out in 1975 it was announced that no one convicted of a scheduled offence committed after February 1976 would be granted special category status, but that the existing privileges of those who had already been granted special category status would not be affected, those who were subsequently convicted of offences committed before March 1976 would also be permitted to claim special category status. At the same time it was announced that prisoners who co-operated would be entitled to remission of half their sentence.[3] By this carefully formulated statement the authorities hoped to avoid any allegation that they had gone back on their word, since potential offenders were given clear advance warning of the change in policy. But the fact that large numbers of prisoners continued to enjoy special category status long after the start of the new regime was clearly an inducement to newly convicted offenders to challenge the new policy.

The Dirty Protest

This challenge was slow to develop, not least because the delays in the legal system meant that no one was convicted of an offence committed after February 1976 until late in 1976. But there was never any doubt that IRA members would continue to demand political status. The first convicted prisoners to be denied special category status refused to wear prison clothes or to work. The authorities responded by charging them with offences against prison discipline, for which they were regularly awarded loss of remission of one week for each week of their protest, three days cellular confinement, and in addition the loss of the privileges of evening association and visits, letter or parcels in excess of the statutory minimum. They were also prevented from wearing their own clothes, and thus forced to wrap themselves in their blankets. It seems clear that this represented a deliberate policy on the part of the prison authorities to induce the protestors to abandon their protest by making life for them as uncomfortable as possible, and by ensuring that they would serve twice as long in prison as they would if they accepted ordinary prison discipline. The policy was not successful. The number of prisoners 'on the blanket' rose steadily and by 1980 was in excess of 300.

It is more difficult to attribute responsibility for the subsequent escalation in the nature of the protest. Soon after the start of their protest the prisoners were told that they would not be allowed to take their blankets out of their cells. As a result the prisoners refused to take advantage of their right to exercise for one hour each day, since that would have meant taking exercise without any clothes or other protection in the middle of winter. They were, however, permitted to use their towels to gird themselves while they went to the washroom, though it had to be removed for use in the washroom. Early in 1977 their application for a second towel for use in washing was rejected. There were also continuing complaints of excessive body searches by prison staff. In response the prisoners refused to leave their cells to wash. Early in 1978 similar problems arose over the use of toilet facilities during the day. The prisoners complained of excessive supervision by prison staff, and in response refused to leave their cells even for that purpose or to take their weekly shower bath. They also began to smear their cells with their own excreta and to break windows and cell furniture. The combination of these various forms of protest is now generally known as the 'dirty protest' which has been maintained in a more or less similar form from March 1978 until the present.

The argument that it was the actions of the authorities rather than of the prisoners which resulted in the escalation of the protest is given some support by the rather different course of events in the women's prison at Armagh. Republican prisoners in Armagh like their colleagues in the Maze refused from the start to accept ordinary prison discipline or to work. Like those in the Maze they were regularly charged with breaches of prison discipline and lost their remission and certain privileges. But since women prisoners are all permitted to wear their own clothes there was no difficulty over exercise. Nor were the protestors denied the privilege of evening association. In practice the protestors were locked in their cells only during working hours.

The situation in Armagh remained stable until February 1980 when the protestors there joined in the dirty protest. Following a disturbance in the course of a general cell search in a wing in which the protestors were held, they were locked in their cells for a full day and were not permitted to use the toilets on the way to their statutory hour of exercise. In response the prisoners adopted the same tactics as had been adopted at the Maze in 1978 of refusing to wash or use the toilets and of smearing their cells with excreta, though they continued to take advantage of their right to an hour's exercise each day and of permission to wear their own clothes. It is difficult to say whether this development at Armagh was the result of a deliberate decision by the prisoners to engineer a disturbance with a view to creating an excuse for joining their colleagues at the Maze. Their supporters alleged that the prisoners were beaten up and 'forced' to adopt the dirty protest by the action of the warders in locking the toilets during the exercise periods immediately following the disturbance. But it is clear that the form of the protest owed more to prior developments at the Maze than to the actions of the authorities.

Proceedings at Strasbourg

As the confrontation between the protesting prisoners and the authorities developed there was increasing public concern over the situation. At first this was restricted to the families of the protesting prisoners and other Republican activists. Provisional Sinn Fein initiated a general political campaign in support of the prisoners' claim to political status and maintained an 'H Block Information Centre' for local and foreign journalists. But a number of other individuals and bodies have from time to time intervened in an attempt to resolve the deadlock and alleviate conditions for the protesting prisoners. In 1977 the Board of Visitors at the Maze Prison asked for a legal opinion on whether the refusal to permit the prisoners to take their statutory exercise except in prison clothes or no clothes at all constituted a breach of the Prison Rules but were advised that it did not. The Roman Catholic Archbishop of Armagh, Cardinal O'Fiaich, attempted on several occasions to mediate between the prisoners and the authorities. And in 1978 a number of protesting prisoners were encouraged to institute proceedings before the European Commission on Human Rights at Strasbourg.

The basis of the prisoners' case was that the actions of the authorities in response to their refusal to accept prison discipline constituted inhuman and degrading treatment or punishment in breach of Article 3 of the European Convention on Human Rights and Fundamental Freedoms. They also claimed interference with their rights of privacy, correspondence and association and of discrimination in comparison with those who were granted special category status before 1976 and with women in Armagh. The British government's case was that all these deprivations were essentially self-inflicted in that they stemmed from the prisoners' refusal to comply with prison rules and regulations which were in themselves reasonable and necessary.

The European Commission after a detailed consideration of submissions from both sides finally decided by a majority in 1980 to declare a major part of the case inadmissible as manifestly ill-founded.[4] It held that while the conditions complained of were clearly inhuman and degrading they were 'self-imposed by the applicants as part of their protest for "special category status" and, were they motivated to improve them, could be eliminated almost immediately'.[5] Only the issues of the prisoners' right to correspondence and of whether their right to complain to the Board of Visitors at the prison or to the Secretary of State provided an effective internal remedy were reserved for further consideration.

The Commission was nonetheless critical of the refusal by the authorities to find a more acceptable solution to the problem posed by the fact that the protestors were clearly not going to change their attitude, and were thus being confined to their cells on a permament basis in conditions which posed a significant threat to their physical and mental well-being:

No doubt the authorities consider that to make concessions to the applicants will result in strengthening their resolve to continue their protest to a successful conclusion. However, the Commission must express its concern at the inflexible approach of the State authorities which has been concerned more to punish offenders against prison discipline than to explore ways of resolving such a serious deadlock. Furthermore, the Commission is of the view that, for humanitarian reasons, efforts should have been made by the authorities to ensure that the applicants could avail of certain facilities such as taking regular exercise in the open air with some form of clothing (other than prison clothing) and making greater use of the prison amenities under similar conditions.[6]

The decision of the European Commission did not resolve the continuing deadlock over the prisoners' demands. In anticipation of the Commission's criticism the authorities offered some concessions to the prisoners early in 1980, notably the opportunity to take their exercise in track suits, to receive extra parcels and to have the use of more cell furniture. But none of these offers were accepted. The protesting prisoners both at the Maze and Armagh continued to demand formal recognition of their political motivation and of the fact that they were not 'ordinary criminals'.

The Struggle for Legitimacy

This brief account of the confrontation over special category status highlights the importance of symbols and labels on all sides of the Northern Ireland conflict.

For the IRA it is vital to assert the legitimacy of their campaign and to emphasise that they are fighting what amounts to a war against Britain as a foreign occupying power in Northern Ireland. The claim for special category status is directly linked to this. It is based on the assertion that the essentially political motivation of those who have committed scheduled offences entitles them to be treated differently from ordinary criminals. The fact that they have been tried in specially constituted courts is an additional argument in favour of some differentiation in treatment. But it is not the central point.

For the authorities it is equally important to insist that those found guilty of scheduled offences are just like ordinary criminals and cannot therefore be entitled to any special treatment in prison. To make any formal concession of separate status to IRA and other paramilitary offenders would, in the current official view, constitute an admission that there is some measure of legitimacy or justification in the campaign by the IRA and its Loyalist counterparts, and encourage those engaged in it to maintain their struggle.

Labelling disputes of this kind are peculiarly impervious to rational argument in that each side believes that the assertion of principles is crucial to the ultimate success of its cause and more important than the alleviation of short term problems. But it is not hard to show that there are serious shortcomings in the arguments on both sides.

In the first place it is quite clear that neither the IRA nor any of its Loyalist counterparts has any valid legal claim to special treatment. The European Commission made a point of emphasising that the admitted political motivation of the applicants in the special category status case did not give them any right in national law or under the European Convention to be treated differently from other convicted offenders. Though the issue was not argued before it the Commission added its opinion that a right to special treatment could not be derived from existing norms of international law.[7] This conclusion would appear to be based on an assessment of the current international conventions on the position of guerrillas under the Geneva Conventions and on the extradition of political offenders.

The Geneva Conventions of 1949 impose on all signatory states a duty to grant all persons affected by, but not actively engaged in, international armed conflicts, including those convicted as rebels, certain basic rights. These include a right to be treated humanely and without any adverse distinction founded on race, colour, religion or faith, sex, birth, or wealth and not to be subjected to outrages on personal dignity or humiliating and degrading treatment.[8] But this does not give those convicted of offences committed in the pursuit of an internal non-international conflict any right to be treated differently from ordinary convicted offenders. That could only be derived from a claim to prisoner-of-war status, which would give protection from punishment during detention and a right to release on the cessation of hostilities. Under the Geneva Conventions of 1949 this may only be claimed by those engaged in an international conflict if they wear an identifiable uniform and carry an identifying mark as combatants, conditions which paramilitaries in Northern Ireland do not meet.

In 1977 two additional Protocols to the Geneva Conventions were drawn up to extend the right of prisoner-of-war status to guerrillas or freedom fighters in both international and non-international conflicts. Though neither of these new Protocols has yet come into force, and neither is therefore binding on the United Kingdom, their very existence is significant. But it is hard to see how the IRA could establish a valid claim under either Protocol.

Protocol I applies only to international armed conflicts. This extends both to cases of declared war or other armed conflict between two or more contracting states, and to conflicts in which 'peoples are fighting against colonial domination and alien occupation and against racist regimes in exercise of their right to self-determination'.[9] To claim combatant status under the Protocol, guerrillas or freedom fighters need only produce their weapons immediately before going into action, carry their arms openly during each military engagement and submit to effective military discipline. It is possible that the IRA could meet these conditions. But it is quite clear that the conflict in Northern Ireland does not meet the other requirements of the Protocol, since the people of Northern Ireland have been granted a formal right of self-determination and have consistently voted by large majorities to maintain the link with Britain.

Protocol II applies to non-international armed conflicts. It affords certain 'fundamental guarantees' to 'all persons who . . . have ceased to take part in hostilities'[10] and provides for minimum standards of treatment for 'persons deprived of their liberty for reasons related to the armed conflict, whether they are interned or detained'.[11] But it does not define combatants who are entitled to prisoner-of-war status, and it does envisage prosecutions for 'criminal offences related to the armed conflict' and provides certain basic safeguards for those who are prosecuted.[12] Even if the IRA could validly claim combatant status for those of its members who are convicted in Diplock courts, it would also have to show that it was a 'dissident armed force or other organised armed group which under responsible command exercised such control over part of a territory as to enable it to carry out sustained and concerted military operations'.[13] Since the Protocol also declares that it is not applicable to 'situations of internal disturbances and tensions, such as riots, isolated and sporadic acts of violence and other acts of a similar nature',[14] it would be very hard to establish that it applied in Northern Ireland.

IRA members have a stronger claim to the status of political offender. Under general international law and under the specific provisions of the Extradition Act 1870 and the European Convention on Extradition of 1957 those who commit offences with political motives are entitled to seek political asylum and to be exempted from extradition. This right has frequently been relied on by IRA members who have fled to the Republic. It is arguable that many would now lose this right under the European Convention on the Suppression of Terrorism of 1977 which provides that fugitive offenders whose crimes involve the use of cruel or vicious means or create a collective danger to human life should generally be extradicted to the country where their offences were committed and should in any event be tried in the country in which they have taken refuge. There is some difference of opinion between Britain and the Republic of Ireland on whether there is a general principle of international law prohibiting extradition for political offences.[15] The view of the British government is that states are free to enter into international agreements which authorise extradition, and it has ratified the European Convention on the Suppression of Terrorism. The official view in the Republic is that its constitution requires it to uphold generally accepted principles of international law and that a bar on extradition for political offences is one such principle. There is more to be said, in our view, for the British than the Irish position on this matter as a question of law. But in any event the legislation passed in both countries following the Sunningdale agreement of 1973 provides for the prosecution in Northern Ireland or Britain of fugitive offenders for offences committed in the Republic and for the prosecution in the Republic of fugitive offenders for terrorist offences committed in Northern Ireland or Britain.[16] The fact that an offence may be classified as a political offence for the purpose of extradition does not therefore free a suspect from prosecution and conviction in either state. Nor does it confer any right to special treatment after conviction.

It is equally clear that in factual terms there are serious deficiencies in the official view on the treatment of paramilitary offenders. In the first place there is no evidence that permitting such offenders not to work and to organise their own activities, whether in compounds or cell blocks, has in practice led to a high propensity to continue with paramilitary activity on release. The records of those appearing in Diplock courts in 1979, analysed in Chapter 3, shows that very few have previous convictions for terrorist activity. If the ill-effects of the compound system were as serious as the Gardiner Committee and others have alleged, many more of those coming before the courts in 1979 would have been expected to be 'graduates' of internment or of special category status. In practice the proportion of those who return to active service on release from prison, whatever conditions they have been held in, is remarkably low.

In the second place the policy of criminalisation which has been pursued by the authorities since 1975 has not in practice reduced the commitment among Republican and Loyalist offenders to the view that they are different from ordinary criminals. This is best illustrated by the extraordinary tenacity of those engaged in the dirty protest. It is also linked to the fact that the IRA and its Loyalist counterparts are essentially communal organisations, in the sense that we have explained in Chapter 3. It does not follow that members of those organisations are entitled to any special treatment while in custody. But there are strong pragmatic grounds for seeking to avoid the kind of adverse publicity and propaganda which has resulted from the attempt to force those who see themselves to be different from ordinary criminals to accept the status of ordinary criminals. There is in any event no criminological evidence to support the now traditional view that prisoners benefit from being required to submit to strict prison discipline and to work. On the contrary there is a growing support for the view that all prisoners, whatever the motivation for their crimes, should be kept in custody in conditions which resemble those outside prison as closely as possible.[17] The requirement to wear a prison uniform, which was originally introduced as much as a means of humiliating prisoners as to facilitate the recapture of escapees,[18] does not advance that aim. This approach does not rule out the provision of work and educational or vocational training programmes for prisoners, nor the offer of early release for those who agree to co-operate in such programmes provided that the rules under which remission is to be granted are clearly established.

For all these reasons we are strongly of the opinion that those who refuse to wear prison clothes or to work should be permitted not to do so, and should not suffer any penalty for their refusal other than the loss of whatever remission in their sentence is granted for participation in educational or vocational programmes or for regular working. The adoption of this policy in Northern Ireland for all prisoners would have the added advantage of showing that the state is prepared to respect deeply held convictions without in any way restricting its right to punish and to detain in custody those who commit serious criminal offences. We know of no evidence that would suggest that such a policy would encourage more people to engage in terrorist activity. On the contrary we believe that a commitment on the part of state authorities to the humane treatment of those who oppose it is more likely to achieve long term stability than a dogged commitment to the principle that no concessions must be made to those who are claiming special category status in the Maze and Armagh prisons.

8. CONCLUSIONS

Conclusions to this study of the use of emergency powers in Northern Ireland may be drawn on a number of different levels. We shall deal first with the implications for current policy in Northern Ireland, then with some more general trends in criminal procedure which are of central importance to the debate on police powers and the right to silence, and finally with the theory and practice of state power.

(a) Policy in Northern Ireland

It is tempting in any account of the operations of the security forces in Northern Ireland to focus on individual incidents in which people have been killed, injured or ill-treated in disputed circumstances. It is important to maintain commitment to civil libertarian values at this basic level. But it is also important to focus attention on broader strategic issues. We have already emphasised in Chapter 3 the extent to which the persistence of the IRA campaign may be linked to the continuing deprivation experienced by some sections of the Catholic population in Northern Ireland. Action on that front remains essential to the restoration of stability. But it would be naive to argue that it is all that is required. While innocent civilians and members of the security forces are being killed and injured and property is being destroyed to the extent which is now current in Northern Ireland some response must be made by the government, if only to avoid the risk of more serious spontaneous violence in reaction. The merits of the various possible responses can perhaps be clarified by identifying four very broad response models: total British withdrawal, the war model, the detention model and the criminal prosecution model.

British Withdrawal

It is easy to make a case for British withdrawal from Northern Ireland. British involvement in Ireland has long been a cause of continuing violence. The record of the British Army and of the British government in dealing with insurrections and disturbances in all parts of Ireland until 1921 and in Northern Ireland since 1969 has been marred by a succession of disreputable and notorious incidents. The British people are in general thoroughly fed up with the whole business and, if given the chance would almost certainly vote for withdrawal by a large majority.

The case against withdrawal is simply that to set a date for British withdrawal before establishing a stable system of government in Northern Ireland which could be expected to maintain itself without British support would risk a much greater upheaval and much greater loss of life than has yet occurred. It is impossible to predict accurately what would happen in any given set of circumstances. But there are some important facts which advocates of withdrawal often ignore. The first is that there are currently some 20,000 armed Protestants in the Ulster Defence Regiment, the RUC and the RUC Reserve. The vast majority of these are committed to the defence of Northern Ireland from what they regard as a Republican threat. When the British Army withdrew in 1920 effective control was handed over to the then equivalent of these forces, which were immediately increased by the creation of the A, B and C Specials to more than 50,000 armed men. Given that the IRA is at present made up of some hundreds of men, perhaps up to a thousand, it is not hard to predict the overall result of a unilateral and rapid British withdrawal in the 1980s. A provisional Protestant government would be established; Catholic enclaves in Belfast and elsewhere would be occupied or encircled; and if there was a serious local Catholic resistance or intervention from the Republic, both of which would seem likely, a civil war on the scale of that experienced in Cyprus or Lebanon would almost certainly ensue.[1]

It would be possible for the British government to attempt to avoid this course of events by making provisions in advance of military withdrawal. One possibility would be to attempt to disarm the existing Protestant forces and to hand over effective control to the Dublin government. It seems highly unlikely that this could be achieved without the situation deteriorating into a civil war. A much more practical alternative would be to hand over legitimate authority and control to the existing Protestant forces, as in the 1920s, and to leave the minority in Northern Ireland to fend for itself. This would clearly cause a major rift with the Irish Republic and possibly with the United States and other countries in Europe. It would in addition be a result which we do not believe that most advocates of unilateral British withdrawal would favour. A third possibility would be to attempt to secure an orderly resettlement of population so that the two communities in Northern Ireland could be effectively separated, leaving the Protestants to form their own smaller state and the Catholics to join with the Republic. This is in theory an attractive option. In practice it would be very difficult to achieve, given the natural commitment of most farmers to retaining their ancestral lands and the huge difficulties which would be caused in trying to resettle up to 250,000 urban Catholics from the Belfast area in the Republic.

We have set out these possibilities in this simple and stark form mainly with a view to encouraging those who argue for British withdrawal to turn their attention to some of the unpleasant realities of the situation in Northern Ireland. In practice we can see little alternative for the British government but to continue with its current policy of maintaining its involvement in, and responsibility for, Northern Ireland until some more stable political settlement can be achieved. For the reasons which we have explained in our Introduction we do not propose to embark on a discussion of the political alternatives. The purpose of this concluding chapter is to analyse the alternative security strategies which might be pursued until a more stable political settlement is achieved.

The War Model

It is often argued that if only the British Army could be freed of the restraints under which it is currently operating in Northern Ireland and permitted to wage all-out war on the IRA the current emergency could be brought to a rapid and satisfactory conclusion. Some support for this view may be taken from the fact that the IRA clearly perceives itself to be fighting a war against the British Army. It is a guerrilla war with some limitation of legitimate targets. It is a war, nonetheless, in which soldiers, policemen and prison officers are shot without warning, and in which bombs and incendiaries are used against all kinds of property, both governmental and private. The use of large-scale car bombs, attacks on railway trains and the like also creates unavoidable risk for the civilian population.

It is not always made clear what the adoption of a war model by the British Army would entail. At the simplest level it would almost certainly involve the adoption of a general policy of shooting suspected terrorists on sight, and the indefinite detention of all captured suspects as prisoners-of-war. Experience in the Irish Republic in the 1920s and in Malaya in the 1950s suggests that it might also involve reprisals against communities from which gunmen or bombers emerged or in which they were sheltered. There is also the possibility of hot pursuit raids into the Republic or even the destruction of suspected terrorist training camps or hideouts. Any or all of these tactics would involve clear breaches of Britain's international obligations under the United Nations Covenant on Civil and Political Rights and the European Convention on Human Rights. Incursions of this kind into the Republic would be of doubtful legality under international law. But recent experience in Rhodesia and Israel suggests that that might not be a determining factor.

It is impossible to say whether the adoption of policies of this kind would be successful in eliminating the IRA. They would be equally likely to cause an escalation in the fighting. And the cost in terms of civilian casualties would certainly be very high. In the period between December 1977 and November 1978 during which the Army appears to have experimented with a 'shoot on sight' policy, three of the ten suspected terrorists who were killed turned out to be totally innocent. The international repercussions would also be very serious. There would almost certainly be diplomatic intervention from the United Nations and other bodies. The risk of military intervention from the Republic, whether official or unofficial, could not be ruled out. Britain might also risk expulsion from the Council of Europe. Considerations like these have always ruled out the adoption of a full-scale war model as a serious policy option.

The Detention Model

A policy of arresting and detaining suspected terrorists without trial may be pursued without resorting to a full-scale war model. This strategy was used between 1971 and 1975, and is still authorised under the Northern Ireland (Emergency Provisions) Act. The current continuation order, approved in July 1980, requires the Secretary of State to seek parliamentary approval for the reintroduction of detention without trial.[2] But there is provision for its temporary adoption in advance of a parliamentary vote if the Secretary of State considers that 'by reason of urgency it is necessary to make the order' without the prior approval of a draft order.[3] There is currently some pressure from some Army and political quarters for the adoption of what is called 'selective internment' against those suspected of planning the continuing IRA campaign and the Loyalist response to it.

There are strong arguments against any return to detention without trial even on a limited basis.

The strongest argument is the evidence of what happened between 1971 and 1975 in terms of military action on the ground. As explained in detail in Chapter 4, the implementation of the policy of putting suspected terrorists behind bars during that period involved the regular and systematic 'screening' of the population in all areas in which there was thought to be a substantial IRA presence. The process of arresting and questioning large numbers of people, sometimes on a street by street basis, inevitably increased the antagonism between the security forces and innocent members of the Catholic communities in which the policy was applied. There is little doubt that it contributed substantially to the flow of recruits into the IRA, and that if a similar policy were reintroduced there would be a similar result, even if the scale of detention was much more limited.

This argument is supported by the statistics on the substantial and continuing decline in the incidence of shootings and bombings since the policy of detention without trial was abandoned, as shown in Table 3.1. There have been variations in the extent and rate of decline. But that there has been a real decrease in the impact of the IRA campaign cannot be denied.

There is also the more general argument that the experience of internment in the period between 1971 and 1975 has so conditioned the Catholic population against any form of detention without trial that its reintroduction would result in a widespread communal reaction and perhaps in a renewed campaign of non-co-operation like the rent and rates strike initiated in 1971. Numerous opinion surveys have established beyond reasonable doubt that most Catholics have a deep-seated objection to detention without trial and a corresponding commitment to the ideals of procedural and substantive criminal justice.[4]

For all these reasons we are satisfied that any return to a policy of detention, and the military security system which would inevitably go with it, would make matters worse, in that it would assist the IRA in recruiting new members and thus in stepping up the level of its campaign.

The Criminal Prosecution Model

Under a pure criminal prosecution model all suspects, whether they were charged with terrorist or ordinary crimes, would be dealt with in ordinary criminal courts and would have a right to jury trial in serious cases. In practice the system of criminal prosecution has been substantially modified in Northern Ireland since 1973 by changes in the common law rules on arrest for questioning and the admissibility of confessions and by the suspension of jury trial, as described in Chapters 5 and 6. But the criminal prosecution model which has been maintained since 1975 remains essentially different from the war or detention models in that a suspect may be kept in custody only if he is charged with a specific criminal offence and the prosecution is able to prove his guilt beyond reasonable doubt.

There are some important consequences of adopting a pure or modified criminal prosecution model. The most important is that some people who are 'known' by the security forces to have committed or organised acts of terrorism will not be put behind bars because there is insufficient evidence to bring them before a court or because a court will not convict them. Relying on criminal prosecution thus makes dealing with suspected terrorists rather like dealing with suspected burglars or pickpockets. No one assumes that all the suspected burglars or pickpockets will be arrested and imprisoned, or that burglary or pick-pocketing will be completely stamped out. The community accepts this as part of the price to be paid for its commitment to the principle that it is better to allow a guilty suspect to go free than to convict an innocent person.

The principal advantage of relying on criminal prosecution in dealing with terrorism is that it helps to avoid the kind of communal distrust and antagonism which the military security and detention policies caused in the period between 1971 and 1975, and conversely that it helps to maintain confidence in the judicial system. In the short term the authorities hope that they will be able to bring sufficient numbers of suspected terrorists before the courts and to obtain a sufficient number of convictions to meet the demands from the bulk of the population for effective action in the face of terrorist attacks and at the same time to diminish support for recruitment by terrorist organisations in their own communities. The longer term objective is to maintain the confidence of the whole population in the organs of the state and general consent to the system of government. In a state like Northern Ireland where there are two communities with potentially divided allegiances and a tradition of support for paramilitary organisations, these considerations are of special importance.

It will already be clear that we support the view that relying on criminal prosecution is the best means of achieving a return to peace and stability in Northern Ireland. Since this has been the policy of successive administrations since the report of the Gardiner Committee in 1975 we are not calling for any basic change in policy. The more difficult issue is whether the modifications in criminal procedure introduced on the recommendation of the Diplock Commission in 1973 were justified and whether they should still be maintained. Our view on this issue is somewhat less clearcut. It would have been better in our view if the authorities had never adopted the policy of detention without trial and the military security system which went with it. Once it had been adopted however, our view was that the primary objective must be to phase it out and that reliance on the Diplock court system was the only practicable means of achieving that end. That was the basis of our evidence to the Gardiner Committee and of our argument in *Law and State*. We remain satisfied that the system of Diplock courts is preferable to detention without trial, and that it has operated without discrimination in cases against Republican and Loyalist defendants. But the risk of error is greater than under the ordinary rules of criminal procedure. And it is clear that modifications in those rules and the abuses which have followed from the elimination of some of the safeguards built into the common law rules have diminished respect for, and confidence in, the judicial system. This is especially true in relation to the rules on interrogation and the admissibility of confessions.

Reforming the Diplock System

There should now in our view be a deliberate and progressive move back towards reliance on the ordinary common law rules of criminal procedure. The risk that a few guilty terrorists might not be convicted who might have been convicted in a Diplock court is a small price to pay for diminishing the risk that a few innocent people will be convicted and for an increase in general acceptance of and confidence in the judicial system. That in its turn will help to diminish support for para-military activity and increase co-operation with the security forces.

The recommendations which we have made in earlier chapters are all designed to assist in achieving these ends. It is sufficient here to give a brief summary of their application to the Army, the police and the courts.

In respect of the Army there should be some clarification of the powers to stop and search and to arrest suspected persons to ensure that these powers are used purely for preventive purposes, as in routine road blocks, and for the arrest of persons reasonably suspected of involvement in unlawful activity. There should be a similar clarification of the power to enter and search occupied houses to ensure that such houses are not searched at night unless a warrant has been obtained on the ground that there is reasonable suspicion that arms or explosives are being held there. Both these recommendations are designed to ensure that the Army does not use its powers for the ulterior purpose of collecting general information on the population in 'suspect' areas. There should also be a deliberate policy of reducing the extent and frequency of Army patrols wherever possible so that its role as a garrison force in support of the police can gradually be restored.

In respect of the police there should be a similar clarification of the power to arrest for questioning to ensure that it is used only in respect of persons reasonably suspected of involvement in terrorist activity. There should also be a statutory code of interrogation practice to govern the conduct of interrogations and provision for the effective disciplining of those responsible for any breach in that code. This could be most effectively achieved by providing for an immediate judicial hearing in any case in which an alleged confession is contested by the defendant with a view to establishing whether there had been a breach of the code of practice.

In respect of the courts the current provisions governing the admissibility of confessions should be repealed and replaced by a provision to the effect that statements obtained during interrogation should be admissible only if it is shown that the statutory code of practice has been complied with. Where the validity of an admissible confession is challenged by the defendant, there should be a requirement of corroboration by some other independent evidence of the guilt of the defendant. Reliance on trial by a single judge should be reduced by excluding robberies not committed for the benefit of terrorist organisations and other less serious offences from the list of scheduled offences. Provision should also be made for the appointment of lay assessors to introduce some element of public participation in Diplock trials.

It must be stressed that all these recommendations are made on the assumption that the system of Diplock courts will be retained only for so long as the level of paramilitary organisation and activity makes it likely that reliance on the ordinary rules of criminal procedure will not achieve an acceptable level of convictions. The only effective means of assessing this in practice is to introduce the kind of measures we have suggested and to monitor the results carefully. For this purpose it is essential to retain the temporary character of any emergency legislation and to require justification for its renewal every six months as is currently provided.

(b) The Reform of Criminal Procedure

Our account of the development and operation of emergency criminal procedures in Northern Ireland has wider implications. Some of the procedures and practices which we have described are already being employed in Britain and elsewhere. Others have been recommended in evidence to the Royal Commission on Criminal Procedure. It is increasingly common, for instance, for persons suspected of serious offences to be held for questioning in police custody and to be denied access to their friends or legal advisers. In some cases the police rely on their powers under the Prevention of Terrorism Act for this purpose. In others they simply assert a power which the vast majority of suspects are not in a position to question either at the time or afterwards. The purpose of this is clearly to induce those held to confess, or otherwise to incriminate themselves. The progressive devaluation of pre-trial proceedings before magistrates, which are now almost exclusively concerned with the issue of bail, and the formalisation of committal proceedings is equally observable in Britain. There are similar pressures on defendants to plead guilty and similar incentives for those who enter into negotiation for that purpose.

It would be inappropriate in this context to attempt a detailed account of these practices in Britain. In most respects they have not yet been developed to the full extent which they have reached in Northern Ireland under the umbrella of the emergency conditions prevailing there. But there can be little doubt that there is a general tendency for the proceedings in the police station to become more significant in respect of the decision on guilt or innocence than those in the courtroom, which are increasingly concerned with the issue of disposal. There is also strong pressure from some quarters for the legalisation of these trends, notably by the adoption of a power for the police to arrest suspects for questioning. Such a power has already been proposed for Scotland in the Criminal Justice (Scotland) Bill 1980.

There are a number of possible responses to these developments from a civil libertarian point of view. It is possibly simply to reassert the traditional approach to the right to silence. We do not think that that is either appropriate or likely to prove effective in preserving civil libertarian values. The trends which we have described have already rendered the supposed right to silence largely illusory in many cases. It is more appropriate in our view to accept that some form of questioning of suspects may properly take place, but to insist that it be conducted under effective legal control. The real need is to eliminate the possibility of interrogation of the kind which has been developed in Northern Ireland and elsewhere.

One possibility, which has already been argued by the National Council for Civil Liberties and others, is to recognise that suspects will be questioned in police stations but to provide that no evidence of that questioning shall be admitted in evidence and that no confession or statement obtained during questioning shall be produced unless it has been taken in the presence of the suspect's legal adviser.[5] The drawback to this approach is that control is asserted over the process of questioning only at the final stage in which the suspect is asked to make a statement. For this reason we prefer the approach which we have suggested in Chapter 5, namely that persons reasonably suspected of serious offences might be required to appear before a magistrate and to submit to, but not necessarily to respond to, relevant questions. One advantage of this procedure would be the assertion of more effective control over police practice at the pre-trial stage, both in respect of the conduct of the questioning and of the decision to call a suspect to questioning. As an alternative a suspect might agree to submit to questioning in the presence of a legal adviser alone. In either case the pressures of isolation and persistent questioning which are designed to break the will of the suspect would be avoided. The failure by a suspect to answer questions would not in itself constitute evidence against him. But as in the case of a refusal by a defendant to give evidence at a trial it would naturally be a factor in the minds of a jury attempting to decide whether it was satisfied beyond reasonable doubt as to the defendant's guilt.

Whichever of these suggestions is pursued, the essential point remains that some action is required to reassert the principle that accused persons should be tried in court, not in the police station. The basic objective must be to ensure that all important parts of the trial process, from initial arrest and questioning to the final verdict and sentence, are subject to effective judicial control. It is not necessary for this purpose to look to continental models of inquisitorial procedure.[6] What is required is the reactivation and modernisation of the various pre-trial judicial procedures, notably the initial appearance before the magistrate and the subsequent committal proceedings, which are already part of the common law tradition but which have become ossified through disuse.

(c) State Power and Civil Liberties

There are three major views on law and its relationship with state power. The most commonly held are the instrumental theory, that the law maintains and perpetuates the position of the ruling class by defining and defending its claim over resources, and the formalist theory, which portrays law as an autonomous system with its own set of substantive and procedural values. There is also increasing interest in the institutional analysis of the various agencies and mechanisms through which the law operates. Our analysis of the operation of the legal system in Northern Ireland over the past ten years shows clearly that none of these on its own provides an adequate explanation.

The view that state power is most clearly expressed in the enforcement of the criminal law, particularly in respect of crimes with a political objective, is widely held. It has also become almost traditional to assert that this was a particularly salient feature of the history of the state of Northern Ireland. In *Law and State* we ourselves expressed the view that 'the legal system by its very constitution is committed to the protection of the existing state' and that 'when that state is threatened the legal system will be used on behalf of the state by those in power in whatever way seems to them most likely to restore stability'.[7] But we also stressed that the internal structures and commitments of the various organs of state, the courts, the police and the army, were different and peculiarly resistant to change, so that what might appear to be a relatively simple matter of the assertion of state power became very much more complex.

We see no reason to alter these views. The assertion of centralised state power has, in a sense, become more difficult under direct rule from Westminster than it was under the Unionist regime. Before 1969 control over the administration of justice was concentrated in the Ministry of Home Affairs at Stormont. Now ultimate authority over all significant political and legislative decisions rests with the British government. But the agencies which must implement those decisions, the courts, the Director of Public Prosecutions, the police and the Army, continue to operate in different ways. They share the same general objectives. But they are committed to different methods of achieving them. The policy makers at the Northern Ireland Office must take into account the likely response of each of these agencies to any given policy. It is convenient at times to talk in terms of British state power in Northern Ireland. But it is important to remember that state power is an abstraction. To understand how it is exercised it is essential to understand the independent contributions of all the various institutions and individuals concerned.

There is an equally widely held view to the effect that state power is exercised through the legal system in the interests of a dominant class. It is not now easy to identify any such dominant class interest in Northern Ireland. Before 1972 there was a direct communal interest in the administration of justice for both the Protestant middle class and the Protestant working classes. Senior positions in the legal profession were occupied for the most part by Protestants from the middle class. But there were also substantial employment opportunities for working class Protestants in the police and the B Specials. The huge expansion in the criminal justice industry since 1969 and the increased commitment under direct rule to non-sectarian recruitment to official posts has greatly increased the range of employment opportunities for middle class Catholics. The legal profession in Northern Ireland, both in terms of private practitioners and in terms of official posts in the Department of Public Prosecutions and the Courts Service, now provides a major source of employment for better-educated Catholics. There has been a corresponding increase in the readiness of middle class Catholics to accept the legitimacy of the state. This may help to explain the noticeable decline in recent years of general criticisms of the administration of justice and specific criticisms of the Diplock court system from the legal profession as a whole and from Catholic lawyers in particular. The only major group which continues to be effectively excluded from the operation of the legal system are working class Catholics who are reluctant to take up positions within the security forces, whether from fear of reprisal at the hands of the IRA or from a general sense of alienation.

It is equally important in our view to focus attention on the ideological as well as the institutional and class factors in the analysis of the administration of the law in Northern Ireland. E.P. Thompson has made the point that law as ideology is ineffective unless its practice is in tune with its rhetoric:

> If the law is partial and unjust, then it will mask nothing, legitimise nothing, contribute nothing to any class hegemony.[8]

This point is relevant to experience in Northern Ireland both before and after the suspension of Stormont in 1972. Before 1972 the failure of successive Unionist governments to guarantee fairness and equality before the law helped to maintain the lack of confidence of a large section of the community in the institutions of the state, and ultimately became the central issue on which the Catholic population mobilised its opposition to the Unionist regime and eventually brought it down. After 1972 the Westminster government sought not only to rely on general appeals to the concepts of justice and fairness but also to draw on the commonsense conceptions of crime and criminality in its attempt to isolate terrorists and legitimise its policy on the treatment of paramilitary offenders in prison. But the very substantial derogations from the traditional conceptions of legal justice and of criminal procedure and the continuing abuses during arrest and interrogation clearly undermined these policies, both during the period of internment and subsequently when the authorities relied exclusively on convictions in Diplock courts. If the practice of the state authorities does not live up to the commitments which they proclaim, their reliance on the legitimising force of the law will achieve nothing.

It does not follow that the ideology of the law and the general acceptance of the concepts of crime and its control through criminal prosecution have no part to play in the resolution of the conflict in Northern Ireland. There is a good deal to be said for the view that where the state is weak, as it is in Northern Ireland, and the power of the government to impose its will is limited, as it is in Northern Ireland, the potential force of legal ideology is all the greater. In the absence of any shared conception of national identity or objective, it is essential for any government in Northern Ireland to build on the general commitment to the civil libertarian values of communal fairness and individual freedom and justice. It is for this reason that we have continued to stress the need for more effective government action to reduce the level of relative deprivation in the Catholic community and to restore the procedural protections which are built into the common law system of criminal justice and which in a very real sense provide the only protection for the individual against the abuse of state power.

Appendix

DRAFT CODE OF INTERROGATION PRACTICE

This code sets out the rules which we propose should govern the interrogation of persons arrested in Northern Ireland under the Northern Ireland (Emergency Provisions) Act 1978 and the Prevention of Terrorism (Temporary Provisions) Act 1976. The code would be added as a schedule to both statutes and would remain in force only for as long as those statutes remained in force. In preparing the draft we have drawn on the recommendations of the Bennett Committee, the existing Judges' Rules and Administrative Directions and the draft Principles for the Protection of all Persons under any form of Detention or Imprisonment published by the United Nations in 1976.

1. Scope of the Code

This code governs the arrest and interrogation of any person deprived of his liberty by virtue of any power contained in either the Northern Ireland (Emergency Provisions) Act 1978 or the Prevention of Terrorism (Temporary Provisions) Act 1976, hereinafter referred to as extraordinary powers of arrest.

2. Procedure on arrest

1. Any person arrested under an extraordinary power of arrest shall be informed at the time of arrest of the reason for the arrest and of the precise power of arrest relied upon.
2. Any constable who arrests without warrant any person whom he reasonably suspects of committing, having committed, or being about to commit a scheduled offence under this act, should do so under the general power of arrest or seizure defined in section 13, unless he has reasonable cause to do otherwise, in which case the reasons for the departure must be stated.

3. Arrest by Her Majesty's forces

Where a person is arrested by a member of Her Majesty's forces under section 14 of the Northern Ireland (Emergency Provisions) Act 1978 he shall not be interrogated for any other purpose than that of establishing his identity.

4. Conduct of interrogation

1. The purpose of interrogation is to confront the person arrested with the suspicions which have led to his arrest and to enable him to be interrogated in connection with those suspicions.

2. No person being interrogated shall be compelled in any circumstance to be a witness against himself.

3. No person being interrogated shall be subjected to the use, or threat of any physical, or psychological violence whatsoever.

4. No person shall be interrogated for a period of more than one hour in any one session and in any event not for more than four hours in any period of twenty-four hours.

5. After each interrogation session the person being interrogated shall be returned to his cell for a period of not less than thirty minutes and shall be supplied with appropriate refreshment.

6. Except for urgent operational reasons no interrogation shall take place between midnight and eight o'clock the following morning.

7. Not more than two police officers shall be present during the interrogation of any person at any one time.

8. Not more than three teams of two officers shall be engaged in the interrogation of any person.

9. Where a person being interrogated is a female no questioning shall take place except in the presence of a woman police officer.

10. At the start of each interrogation session the police officers engaged in the interrogation shall inform the person being interrogated of their names and official numbers; any other police officer or other person who enters the interrogation room shall be similarly identified.

11. At the start of each interrogation session the person being interrogated shall be cautioned in the following terms:

    'You are not obliged to say anything unless you wish to do so, but what you say may be put into writing and given in evidence.'

12. When a person being interrogated informs those interrogating him that he wishes to make a written statement that statement shall be taken in accordance with Rule IV of the Judges' Rules.

13. Where an arrested person has been charged he shall forthwith be cautioned in the following terms:

    'Do you wish to say anything? You are not obliged to say anything unless you wish to do so, but whatever you say will be taken down in writing and may be given in evidence.'

Any further questioning relating to the offences for which he has been charged shall be strictly in accordance with Rule III(b) of the Judges' Rules.

5. Treatment of persons arrested as a consequence of the exercise of an extraordinary power of arrest

A person detained as a consequence of the exercise of an extraordinary power of arrest shall:

1. have the right to regular meals and refreshments and reasonable opportunities for exercise and sleep at normal hours; and
2. have the right to be medically examined and treated as soon as practicable after his arrest, and in no circumstances later than four hours after the arrest, at any other time during his detention and immediately prior to his charging or release; where practicable and if requested such medical examination and treatment shall be carried out by the person's own doctor or another doctor nominated by him.

6. *Access by friends, relatives and legal advisers*

A person detained as a consequence of the exercise of an extraordinary power of arrest shall:

1. have the right to have any two persons nominated by him informed of his arrest and of his place of detention as soon as practicable after his arrest; and
2. have the right to be visited by any person nominated by him for a period of thirty minutes in each twenty-four hours of detention. Any such visit may take place in the presence of a police officer; and
3. have the right to see a solicitor of his own choosing at his own request or the request of a friend or relative at any time after twenty-four hours after his initial arrest. Any such visit may take place in the sight of but not the hearing of a police officer.

7. *Records*

1. A contemporary written record shall be maintained from the time of arrest, detailing the time of arrest, the time and duration of all interrogation sessions, of the time and duration of medical examinations and medical treatment, of the time and duration of visits from friends, relatives and legal advisers, and of the time and nature of all meals and refreshments.
2. A copy of this record shall be made available on request to the person arrested or to his legal adviser.

8. *Children, young persons and mentally handicapped persons*

1. A child or young person arrested under an extraordinary power of arrest shall be interrogated only in the presence of a parent or guardian or, if it is not practicable to secure the attendance of a parent or guardian, in the presence of a person who is not a police officer and is of the same sex as the child or young person.
2. When a police officer becomes aware that a person arrested under an extraordinary power of arrest has a mental handicap, no further interrogation of that person shall take place except in the presence of a parent or other person in whose care, custody or control he is or, if it is not practicable to secure the attendance of such a person, in the presence of a person who is not a police officer and is of the same sex as the person arrested.

9. Admissibility of evidence

No statement or admission, whether written or oral, made by a person arrested under an extraordinary power of arrest nor any other evidence as to his conduct during interrogation shall be admitted in subsequent criminal proceedings against that person unless it is established beyond reasonable doubt, the proof of which shall lie on the prosecution, that the provisions of this Code have been complied with.

10. Enforcement

A judge of the High Court of Northern Ireland shall have jurisdication to hear an application for an injunction to enforce any of the provisions of this Code and to award damages for any breach of the provisions of this Code.

FOOTNOTES

CHAPTER 1

1. T. Hadden and P. Hillyard, *Justice in Northern Ireland: A Study in Social Confidence*, Cobden Trust, 1973.
2. K. Boyle, T. Hadden and P. Hillyard, *Law and State: The Case of Northern Ireland*, Martin Robertson, 1975.
3. M. Tomlinson, *Policing the Periphery — Ideologies of Repression in Northern Ireland*, Bulletin on Social Policy, No.5, 1980, p.24; for a defence of a civil libertarian position see E.P. Thompson, *A Secret State* in *Writing by Candlelight*, Merlin Press, 1980.

CHAPTER 2

1. R.J. Lawrence and S. Elliot, *The Northern Ireland Border Poll*, HMSO (London), 1975.
2. Report of the Commission on Disturbances in Northern Ireland, Cmd.532, HMSO (Belfast), 1969 (Cameron Report).
3. Standing Advisory Commission on Human Rights, *The protection of human rights by law in Northern Ireland*, Cmnd.7009, HMSO (London), 1977.
4. Northern Ireland Office, *Discussion Paper: Finance and the Economy*, HMSO (London), 1977.
5. These figures are taken from the regular press releases issued by the Department of Manpower Services for Northern Ireland.
6. Northern Ireland Housing Executive, *Belfast Household Survey 1978*, 1979, Table 25.
7. Northern Ireland Community Relations Commission, *Flight: a report on population movement in Belfast*, 1971.
8. P. Bew, P. Gibbon and H. Patterson, *The State in Northern Ireland 1921-72*, Manchester University Press, 1979, pp.165-168.
9. *Belfast — Areas of Special Need*, HMSO (Belfast), 1976; E. Evason, *Ends that won't meet: a study of poverty in Belfast*, Child Poverty Action Group, 1980.
10. *Belfast Household Survey 1978*, Table 10.
11. B. Black *et al.*, *Low Pay in Northern Ireland*, Low Pay Unit, 1980.
12. *Belfast Household Survey 1978*, Table 19.

Further Reading

Northern Ireland Housing Executive, *Northern Ireland Household Survey 1975*, 1976.

F.W. Boal, *The Spatial Distribution of Some Social Problems in the Belfast Urban*

Area, Northern Ireland Community Relations Commission, 1974.

F.W. Boal, *Territoriality and Class: a study of two residential areas in Belfast,* Irish Geography (1971), Vol.6, No.3, pp.229-248.

A.E.C.W. Spencer, *Ballymurphy: a tale of two surveys,* Department of Social Studies, Queen's University of Belfast, 1973.

L. Taylor and S. Nelson (eds.), *Young People and Civil Conflict in Northern Ireland,* Department of Health and Social Services (Belfast), 1978.

R. Wiener, *The Rape and Plunder of the Shankill,* Farset Co-operative Press, 2nd. ed., 1980.

CHAPTER 3

1. Northern Ireland Community Relations Commission, *Intimidation in Housing,* 1974.
2. Report of Tribunal of Inquiry on Violence and Civil Disturbances in Northern Ireland in 1969, Cmd.566, HMSO (Belfast), 1972 (Scarman Report).
3. J. Bowyer Bell, *The Secret Army,* Anthony Blond, 1970; T.P. Coogan, *The IRA,* Fontana, 1980.
4. K. Boyle, R. Chesney and T. Hadden, *Who are the Terrorists, Fortnight* Issue No.126, 1976; *New Society,* 6 May 1976.
5. D. Boulton, *The UVF 1966-1973: An Anatomy of Loyalist Rebellion,* Gill and Macmillan, 1973.

Further Reading

F. Burton, *The Politics of Legitimacy: Struggles in a Belfast Community,* Routledge and Kegan Paul, 1978.

G. Bell, *The Protestants of Ulster,* Pluto Press, 1976.

F. Wright, *Protestant Ideology and Politics in Ulster,* Archives Europeennes de Sociologie (1973), Vol.XIV.

W.D. Flackes, *Northern Ireland: a political directory 1968-79,* Gill and Macmillan, 1980.

CHAPTER 4

1. Report of a Committee to consider, in the context of civil liberties and human rights, measures to deal with terrorism in Northern Ireland, Cmnd.5847, HMSO (London), 1975 (Gardiner Report).
2. F. Kitson, *Low Intensity Operations,* Faber & Faber, 1971; K. McGuffin, *The Guineapigs,* Penguin Books, 1974.
3. Report of the Commission to consider legal procedures to deal with terrorist activities in Northern Ireland, Cmnd.5185, HMSO (London), 1972 (Diplock Report), para.49-50.
4. Report of the Committee of Inquiry into Police Interrogation Procedures in Northern Ireland, Cmnd.7497, HMSO (London), 1979, para.70 (Bennett Report); see further Chapter 5.
5. *Ibid.,* Appendix I.
6. See generally Review of the operation of the Prevention of Terrorism (Temporary Provisions) Acts 1974 and 1976, Cmnd.7324, HMSO (London), 1978 (Shackleton Report).
7. Northern Ireland Information Service, Press Release, 1979.
8. *Ibid.,* para.66.
9. *D.P.P. v Adams,* Northern Ireland Judgment Bulletin, September 7, 1978, Belfast City Commission.
10. See generally *Attorney General for Northern Ireland's Reference (No.1 of 1975)* (1976) 3 Weekly Law Reports 235.

Further Reading

C. Ackroyd, K. Margolis, J. Rosenhead and T. Shallice, *The Technology of Political Control,* Penguin Books, 1977.

D. Campbell, *Society under Surveillance,* in P. Hain (ed.), *Policing the Police,* Vol. 2, John Calder, 1980.

T. Bunyan, *The Political Police in Britain,* Julian Friedmann, 1976.

CHAPTER 5

1. Report of the enquiry into allegations against the security forces of physical brutality in Northern Ireland arising out of events on the 9th August 1971, Cmnd.4823, HMSO (London), 1971 (Compton Report); *Ireland v. United Kingdom of Great Britain and Northern Ireland* (Application No.5310/71), Report of the European Commission on Human Rights (adopted 25th January 1976) and Judgment of the European Court of Human Rights (delivered on 18th January 1978); Report of the Committee of Inquiry into Police Interrogation Procedures in Northern Ireland, Cmnd.7497, HMSO (London), 1979 (Bennett Report).

2. *R. v. Corr* (1968) Northern Ireland Reports 193.

3. Judges Rules and Administrative Directions to the Police, HMSO (London), 1976; revised version, 1980.

4. Compton Report, *supra.*

5. See the Report of the European Commission on Human Rights in *Ireland v. United Kingdom of Great Britain and Northern Ireland, supra.,* pp.222-475.

6. Report of the Committee of Privy Counsellors appointed to consider authorised procedures for the interrogation of persons suspected of terrorism, Cmnd.4901, HMSO (London), 1972 (Parker Report).

7. H.C. Deb., Vol.832, col.743 (2 March 1972).

8. *Ireland v. United Kingdom of Great Britain and Northern Ireland, supra.*

9. Northern Ireland Judgment Bulletin, May 1972, Belfast City Commission; the decision was criticised in the Diplock Report, para.83; see also D. Greer, *Admissibility of Confessions and the Common Law in times of Emergency* (1973) 24 *Northern Ireland Legal Quarterly* 199.

10. During the debates on the Northern Ireland (Emergency Provisions) Bill the Attorney General stated that 'there had been 55 abandoned cases, nolle prosequis, in Belfast since the beginning of 1972 because of the inadmissibility of confession statements', H.C. Deb., Vol.855, col.388 (17th April 1973).

11. Report of the Commission to consider legal procedures to deal with terrorist activities in Northern Ireland, Cmnd.5185, HMSO (London), 1972 (Diplock Report), para.87.

12. *Ibid.,* para.89.

13. *Ibid.,* para.84.

14. The current provision is the Prevention of Terrorism (Temporary Provisions) Act 1976, s.12.

15. Bennett Report, *supra.,* para.46; see also P. Taylor, *Beating the Terrorists: Interrogation at Omagh, Gough and Castlereagh,* Penguin Books, 1980.

16. Bennett Report, *supra.,* Appendix 2.

17. Report of an Amnesty International Mission to Northern Ireland, 1978.

18. Bennett Report, *supra.,* para.404(16).

19. Action to be taken on the recommendations of the Committee of Inquiry into Interrogation Procedures in Northern Ireland, Northern Ireland Office, 29th June, 1979.

20. Bennett Report, *supra.*, Appendix I.
21. *Ibid.*, Appendix I.
22. W. Sargant, *Battle for the Mind,* Heinemann, 1957. A.M.P. Kellam, A Convincing False Confession, *New Law Journal* January 10, 1980.
23. W. Sargant, *The vital interrogation question: just how voluntary is a voluntary confession?, The Times,* 26 May, 1980.
24. Report of Enquiry by Sir Henry Fisher into the death of Maxwell Confait, HMSO (London), 1977.
25. Report on the European Commission on Human Rights in *Ireland v. United Kingdom of Great Britain and Northern Ireland, supra.,* p.376.
26. *R. v. McCormick* [1977] Northern Ireland Reports 105; see also *R. v. Milne* [1978]. Northern Ireland Reports 110, in which it was held that a confession obtained after 39 hours of interrogation should not be admitted because the suspect was confused.
27. Bennett Report, *supra.,* para.156; in the period from July 1978 to June 1980 there were a further four cases in which the Director of Public Prosecutions declined to prosecute on similar grounds.
28. See also Bennett Report, *supra.,* para.84.
29. *Ibid.,* para.101.
30. *R. v. Smith,* unreported, May 1979, Belfast City Commission.
31. *R. v. McCaul,* unreported, December 1979, Belfast City Commission; an appeal against the conviction was dismissed.
32. Police Complaints Board for Northern Ireland, Annual Report 1979, HMSO (Belfast), 1980.
33. Royal Ulster Constabulary, Chief Constable's Report 1978, Table 4.6.
34. Bennett Committee, *supra.,* para.157; between 1972 and the end of 1978 19 officers were prosecuted (one of them twice) in respect of eight separate incidents; of these 16 were found not guilty at first instance; in one case a plea of *nolle prosequi* was entered; in the remaining two cases the officers were convicted at first instance but their convictions were set aside on appeal.
35. *Ibid.,* Chapter 12.
36. See above, note 19.
37. Under the Metropolitan Police Courts Act 1839, s.24 persons found in possession of stolen goods could be convicted of an offence unless they gave a convincing account of how they came into possession (the section was repealed in 1977); under the Prevention of Crime Act 1953 it is an offence to carry an offensive weapon without lawful authority or reasonable excuse and it is up to the accused to show that he has such authority or excuse.
38. Bankruptcy Act 1914, s.15; Companies Act 1948, s.167 (which permits *any person* to be required to attend court and answer relevant questions before a judge.
39. Prevention of Terrorism (Temporary Provisions) Act 1976, s.12; Criminal Justice (Scotland) Bill, cl.2.
40. *Supra.,* para.2.26.
41. *Ibid.,* paras.2.19-2.23.
42. National Council of Civil Liberties, Submission to the Royal Commission on Criminal Procedure, 1979, Part 4.
43. *Ibid.,* para.2.22.
44. Justice, *Pre-Trial Criminal Procedure: Police Powers and the Prosecution Process,* 1979, para.25.
45. *Ibid.,* para.41.

Further Reading

11th Report of the Criminal Law Revision Committee, Cmnd.4991, 1972.
Report of a Committee on the Feasibility of an Experiment in the Tape-Recording

117

of Police Interrogations, Cmnd.6630, HMSO (London), 1976.

M. Mander, *The Right to Silence in the Police Station and the Caution* in P. Glazebrook (ed.) *Reshaping the Criminal Law,* Stevens, 1978.

Kennedy Lindsay, *Ambush at Tullywest,* Dunrod Press, 1979, Ch.17.

CHAPTER 6

1. Report of the Commission to consider legal procedures to deal with terrorist activities in Northern Ireland, Cmnd.5185, HMSO (London), 1972 (Diplock Report), paras.17, 35-38, 73-92.
2. Northern Ireland (Emergency Provisions) Act 1973, Schedule 4.
3. Northern Ireland (Emergency Provisions) (Amendment) Act 1975, Schedule 2.
4. T. Hadden and S. Wright, *'A terrorist trial in Crumlin Road',* New Society, 28 June 1979.
5. Criminal Statistics, England and Wales 1978, Cmnd.7670, HMSO (London), 1979.
6. Northern Ireland (Emergency Provisions) Act 1978, s.21.
7. *Ibid.,* s.2.
8. *Ibid.,* s.3.
9. Prosecution of Offences (Northern Ireland) Order 1972, implementing the recommendations of the Report of the Working Party on Public Prosecutions, Cmd.554, HMSO (Belfast), 1971 (MacDermott Report).
10. Speech at Queen's University, Belfast, October 16, 1979.
11. J. Baldwin and M. McConville, *Negotiated Justice,* Martin Robertson, 1977.
12. J. Baldwin and M. McConville, *The Influence of the Sentencing Discount in Inducing Guilty Pleas,* · in J. Baldwin and A.K. Bottomley (eds.) *Criminal Justice: Selected Readings,* Martin Robertson, 1978.
13. See *'A terrorist trial in Crumlin Road',* note 4 above.
14. *R. v. Smyth, Murray and Culbert,* unreported, 12 December 1979, Belfast City Commission.
15. *R. v. Smith,* unreported, May 1979, Belfast City Commission.
16. Report of the Committee of Inquiry into Police Interrogation Procedures in Northern Ireland, Cmnd.7497, HMSO (London), 1979 (Bennett Report), para.202.
17. J. Baldwin and M. McConville, *Jury Trials,* Oxford University Press, 1979, Ch.1.
18. Standing Advisory Commission on Human Rights, Annual Report for 1978-79, (1980), para.17.
19. *Supra.,* pp.90-91.

Further Reading

S. McCabe and R. Purves, *By-Passing the Jury,* Blackwell, 1972.

Law and Society Review, Special Issue on Plea Bargaining, Vol.13, No.2 (1979).

Prosecutions in Northern Ireland: a study of facts, HMSO (London), 1974.

CHAPTER 7

1. Report on the Administration of the Prison Service 1972-1976, HMSO (Belfast), 1977; current figures supplied by the Northern Ireland Information Service.
2. Report of a Committee to consider, in the context of civil liberties and human rights, measures to deal with terrorism in Northern Ireland, Cmnd. 5847, HMSO (London), 1975 (Gardiner Report), paras.105-107.

3. Prison (Amendment) Rules (Northern Ireland) 1976; see also Treatment of Offenders (Northern Ireland) Order 1976.
4. *McFeeley v. United Kingdom* (Application No.8317/78), Partial Decision of the European Commission on Human Rights (adopted 15 May 1980).
5. *Ibid.,* p.84.
6. *Ibid.,* p.86.
7. *Ibid.,* p.81.
8. Art.3(1).
9. Art.1.
10. Art.4.1.
11. Art.5.1 and 5.2.
12. Art.6.
13. Art.1.
14. Art.2.
15. Report of the Law Enforcement Commission, Cmnd.5627, HMSO (London), 1974; see also C. Symmons, (1978) *Irish Jurist,* pp.36-66.
16. The United Kingdom statute is the Criminal Jurisdiction Act 1975; the Irish statute is the Criminal Law (Jurisdiction) Act 1976.
17. Committee of Inquiry into the United Kingdom Prison Services, Cmnd.7673, HMSO (London), 1979 (May Report).
18. The Prison Act of 1779 (19 Geo.III c.74 s.35), provided that prisoners 'be clothed with a coarse and uniform apparel with certain obvious marks or badges affixed to the same as well as to humiliate the wearers as to facilitate discovery in case of escape'.

Further Reading

T.P. Coogan, *On the Blanket: The H Block Story,* Ward River Press, 1980.

CHAPTER 8

1. Conor Cruise O'Brien, *States of Ireland,* Hutchinson, 1972.
2. Northern Ireland (Emergency Provisions) Act 1978 Continuance Order 1980.
3. Northern Ireland (Emergency Provisions) Act 1978, s.33.
4. *Law and State, supra.,* p.145.
5. National Council of Civil Liberties, *Submission to the Royal Commission on Criminal Procedure,* 1979, Part 4.
6. National Association for the Care and Resettlement of Offenders, *Inquisitorial Systems of Justice,* 1980.
7. *Law and State, supra.,* pp.1-3.
8. E.P. Thompson, *Whigs and Hunters,* Penguin Books, 1977, p.263.

Further Reading

R. Rose, *Northern Ireland: a time of choice,* Macmilllan, 1976.
M. Farrell, *The Orange State,* Pluto Press, 1980.
B. Fine, R. Kinsey, J. Lea, S. Piciotto and J. Yound (eds.), *Capitalism and the Rule of Law,* Hutchinson, 1979.

The Cobden Trust is a registered charity, established in 1963 to undertake research and education work in the field of civil liberties. It seeks the protection and extension of civil liberties in the United Kingdom and has a two fold strategy to achieve this objective: research, into the causes of injustice, and education work, informing the public about their rights and responsibilities.

How you can help

While we are able to raise funds from charitable trusts and foundations, we depend also on generous public support. As a registered charity, the Trust can recover tax from the Inland Revenue on any covenanted donation. If you would like to help us in this way or would like further information, then please write for details to the Secretary, the Cobden Trust, 186 Kings Cross Road, London WC1X 9DE.